I0450143

INTIMATE
LISTENING

By Bonnie Jacobson, Ph.D.

Love Triangles
If Only You Would Listen
The Shy Single
Lasting Love (working title)

INTIMATE LISTENING

SEVEN STEPS TO CONNECT TO THE HEART AND SOUL OF THE ONE YOU LOVE

BONNIE JACOBSON, PH.D.
WITH GUY KETTELHACK

Author Choice Press
New York Bloomington

Intimate Listening
Seven Steps to Connect to the Heart
and Soul of the One You Love

Copyright © 1995, 2008 Bonnie Jacobson

All rights reserved. No part of this book may be used or reproduced by
any means, graphic, electronic, or mechanical, including photocopying,
recording, taping or by any information storage retrieval system
without the written permission of the publisher except in the case
of brief quotations embodied in critical articles and reviews.

The views expressed in this work are solely those of the author
and do not necessarily reflect the views of the publisher, and the
publisher hereby disclaims any responsibility for them.

Originally published by St. Martin's Press,
175 Fifth Avenue, New York, N.Y. 10010

Authors Choice Press
an imprint of iUniverse
iUniverse books may be ordered through booksellers or by contacting:

iUniverse
1663 Liberty Drive
Bloomington, IN 47403
www.iuniverse.com
1-800-Authors (1-800-288-4677)

Because of the dynamic nature of the Internet, any Web addresses or links
contained in this book may have changed since publication and may no longer be
valid. The views expressed in this work are solely those of the author and do not
necessarily reflect the views of the publisher, and the publisher hereby disclaims
any responsibility for them.

ISBN: 978-1-4401-1006-1 (pbk)

Printed in the United States of America

iUniverse rev. date: 12/22/2008

The characters in this book are composed of amalgamations of aspects of myself, of my imagination, and partial mannerisms of other people I have known.

BONNIE JACOBSON, PH.D.

CONTENTS

Acknowledgments · IX

Introduction: ENDING THE WAR · 1

Preliminaries: START WITH "ME," NOT "WE" · 7

Step One: RECOGNIZING TENSION · 29

Step Two: CROSSING THE STREET · 45

Step Three: ENGAGING THE OUTER EAR · 69

Step Four: ACTIVATING THE INNER EAR · 87

Step Five: REACHING FOR THE PAST · 103

Step Six: EMPATHIZING THROUGH
DETACHMENT · 121

Step Seven: BUILDING A BRIDGE · 139

Index · 155

ACKNOWLEDGMENTS

It's gratifying to have the opportunity to say thank you publicly and permanently to those who have contributed so much to this book. I only hope I can give some evidence here of how much I appreciate what these contributions have meant to me.

I wish, first, to acknowledge the Creator of us all who has given me the health and the imagination to uncover a solution that truly brings happiness to unhappy couples.

I must thank every couple who has come to see me in the last twenty-three years. The privilege of working with these men and women, the lessons they have taught me, their frustrations, pain, love, and breakthroughs constitute the essential source of the insights of this book.

I wish to acknowledge Guy Kettelhack. He is more than my writing partner; he is the father of this creation, as I am the mother.

Kudos to Lynn Sonberg and Meg Schneider, whose brilliant structural suggestions and expertise as literary agents were essential to the conception of the book and its publication.

Barbara Anderson, our editor at St. Martin's, has been a model of precision and professionalism; her sensitive support and suggestions led to a very rapid gestation and birth of this ''baby.''

Now, to acknowledge those in my personal life: First, my sister, Suzanne Stutman, a brilliant psychologist, writer, and media educator who for most of my adult life has listened to, supported, corrected, and improved my written and professional work.

My brother, Dr. Raymond Singer, an innovative neurotoxocologist who has taught me how to listen to my body, to the environment, and (following his example) to listen to the beat of my own drum.

Dr. Linda Carter, my soulmate, who has put up with me for twenty-eight years—even before I learned the seven steps.

My mentor and cherished friend Dr. Bonnie Maslin—her husband, Dr. Yehuda Nir, calls us "the generic Bonnies"—has been a generous, abundant source of who's who and what's what in the business of writing books, as well as TV and radio appearances.

My husband, Arie, has taught me how to be fearless, tenacious, and unaccepting of defeat. His belief in me and his support have given me the courage to reach for the best of which I'm capable.

My sons, Eric and Brad Jacobson, have taught me how to listen in two ways: through their nonnegotiable demands that I listen to them, and, even more important, by their own example as good listeners, a gift for which they have a natural talent.

And finally, much gratitude to my mother, Rose Singer—the best listener I have ever known.

PREFACE TO
INTIMATE LISTENING.

Why republish <u>If Only You Would Listen</u> with iUniverse and then rename the book <u>Intimate Listening</u>? Well the answer lies in the life of the listening book over the last decade. In the therapy room, when coaching my clients how to use this technique, it became apparent that when a listener took the time to follow the seven steps to hearing out the other person's perspective a magical intimacy, compassion, and warmth appeared. Connecting to the heart and soul of another triggers a feeling of love in the listener and increases the receptivity of the speaker. I have noted that when the speaker is finished with her side of a situation she is much more receptive to the former listener's perspective. Therefore the new title *Intimate listening—connecting to the heart and soul of someone you love* just wrote itself into existence.

And why to republish at all? I have noticed that <u>If Only You Would Listen</u> has become more useful to more and more people as the years progress. It was born during the booming 90's when listening was not a very high priority. We had our prosperity, peace, and contentment. Then 9/11 happened, next the Iraq war and now the complete economic downturn.

If giving and receiving love was important in the 90's it is the essential vehicle for happiness in the first decade of the 21st century. Instead of life becoming more secure, peaceful, easier for all people, it has become uncertain with less possibility of **things** being accessible and therefore important in our lives.

Luckily <u>Intimate Listening</u> does not cost money. It just costs time. To do it properly you must be willing to quiet your mind and sit still long enough to truly hear what the other person is trying to get at. Once that happens it becomes much easier to build a bridge from where you are to where the other is coming from. Think of a river. You are on one side and the speaker is on the other side. After you find out exactly where on the other side of the river the speaker is located you can then place your bridge over to his spot. You do this by telling your side of the story in his language.

Why iUniverse instead of a more traditional publisher for round two? Well, first, I am in the process of writing a sequel to Intimate Listening that defines the components that we can choose to elect if lasting love is our goal. And with the current state of the world, lasting love is more important than ever before. This new book is to be published in 2010 by Adam's Media. Second, iUniverse is an efficient, affordable method for insuring that how to listen is accessible to all people, everywhere, whenever they care to reach for it through the internet.

All 10,000 books that were originally published by St. Martin's press are located in someone's book collection around the United States.

My own patients are asking for books and I have no more left, thus the need to republish is pressing.

So to my new readers: please get as much pleasure out of the results of this book as I have had in helping thousands of couple's learn how to truly listen to the heart and soul of someone they love.

Peace and contentment to all of us.

Dr. Bonnie Jacobson
drbonniejacobson@aol.com
website: drbonniejacobson.com

INTIMATE
LISTENING

INTRODUCTION

ENDING THE WAR

"HE NEVER OPENS UP." "SHE NEVER LISTENS."

These complaints point to the most common dilemma I've heard from the scores of men and women with whom I've worked as a psychotherapist over the past three decades: not being able to communicate with the one you love. Communication blocks between men and women are endemic. Despite all the attention this issue has received, most spouses and lovers don't seem to be any better at getting through to each other now than they ever were.

I'm certainly not the first to observe the frustration and despair that afflict so many people in love relationships—the pain of not being able to connect emotionally with the one person you want most to reach. Magazine articles, TV and radio talk shows, and self-help books are full of suggestions concerning "How to Get Him/Her to Listen." The problem is that, even with more thoughtful attempts to address this problem, most of the advice is based on stereotypes and is therefore too limited and general to be truly helpful. All too often, women are told that men are a cross between infants and Mack trucks: treat their fragile egos gently, but accept that they can't help being blunt, rude, and macho. When a man is told anything about a woman other than how to pick her up (see any current men's magazine), it's generally a list of

1

quick-fix tips: bring her flowers, take her out to dinner, make her think you're listening to her, and the standard greeting card: "Tell her that you love her."

Unfortunately, we are often sidetracked by the excess of misinformation about men's and women's communication blocks. Our entire culture seems, sometimes, to conspire against us with sweeping, sexist generalizations that obscure rather than illuminate the personal and idiosyncratic approaches we take to communicating. Assumptions like "Men never talk" or "Women talk too much"—still promoted by many books and magazine articles about communication between the sexes—harm us, divide us. While there are certainly some common, culturally learned differences between what is thought of as the traditional male and the traditional female styles of communication, by no means are *all* men and women locked into these culturally determined agendas, or to the same degree. In fact, very often in my practice I find that a wife will communicate more in what is thought of as the typical "male" pattern and the husband in the typical "female" pattern. In 1969 I studied these differences in what are called classic value patterns—patrism (the male pattern) and matrism (the female). What I discovered is that choosing one pattern over the other is determined more by childhood value patterns than by gender.

Men's and women's communication styles cover a phenomenally wide range. The individual communication patterns we each bring to any love relationship are almost always more subtle and complex than the stereotypical "aggressive man" or "passive woman" models too many writers and therapists have proposed. There's simply a lot more going on, both consciously and unconsciously, than these assumptions suggest.

In addition to the idiosyncratic challenges to communication each of us faces as individuals, there is one much more massive and general obstacle, faced equally by men and women: the urge to blame. Our culture encourages us to take sides quickly, to arm and defend ourselves against the other guy. We are taught by many politicians, journalists, TV talk show emcees, and other media personalities to blame first, ask questions later. Find a scapegoat before someone pins the blame on *you*. The emphasis isn't on understanding or empathy; it's on finding who's at "fault."

What has all of this done to us? It certainly hasn't brought us closer together. Blame isolates. In the wake of accusation, you find yourself feeling abandoned, as if on a desert island with nowhere to go and nothing but anger for a companion. It takes work to realize that, in intimate miscommunication, no one is to "blame." No partner is ever flatly right or wrong, because each partner has a unique field of perception, of reality.

Overcoming Intimate Miscommunication

Over the course of my thirty years as a psychologist, I have developed a seven-step communication process that is easy and enjoyable to use, that *encourages* communication between the sexes, and that has proved effective even in the most difficult relationships. The Seven Steps to Intimate Communication are based on close, penetrating observations of how couples and families communicate and miscommunicate; its process is not simplistic: the steps go deep. In fact, if you follow them closely, you will change more than your ability to hear and be heard by your partner. You will change—and improve—the basic ways you and your lover or spouse understand and relate to each other.

Accomplishing this isn't a matter of finding devious ways to trick your partner into being honest or coerce him into listening to you. A woman doesn't have to learn about football and cars to be able to talk to her "man." Men don't have to learn a new "feminine" vocabulary to get through to women. Perhaps the biggest surprise about the solution I offer in this book is that communication requires allowing you and your partner to be *more* of who you both are, not less.

Doing this means accomplishing two major tasks:

1. Learning about your own motivations so that you can begin to distance yourself from some of the reflexive reactions that block your ability to hear, or to speak to, your partner—in other words, **get beyond the urge to blame.** Once you've spent some time examining your own behavior patterns, you're in a better position to hear your partner. It's at this point, after you have begun to observe some of your habitual defenses, in effect holding up a mirror so that you can see yourself more clearly, that you can face the second task, which is to

2. **Deconstruct your partner's language.** This involves listening to and understanding the words your partner is saying rather than what you *think* he or she means. Exploring this constitutes the bulk of the program in *If Only You Would Listen.* As you'll learn, you accomplish this deconstruction by focusing on your partner's words and sentence structure, feeding back what he or she says in a way that will help both of you to understand what lies beneath the surface of his or her words.

This approach is based partly on the work of George Kelly, a social psychologist in the 1950s who wrote *The Psychology of Personal Constructs* (Norton, 1955). Kelly discovered that a person's specific choice of words reveals his or her "personal construct": our strings of sentences hold the key to how we perceive reality. The seven steps you'll learn here will help you to unravel these strings so that you understand more of what your partner is really saying. Once you realize that more is going on beneath your partner's words than either of you realized, and that what you may once have perceived as a personal attack usually has little or nothing to do with you (based, as it usually is, on childhood patterns that long predate your relationship), your own defensive tension decreases even more. You'll both be able to overcome your reflexive responses. The result? You become a more objective—and less threatening—listener; your partner feels safer and thus becomes more open and revealing.

Most of the couples I've worked with have found the Seven Steps to Intimate Communication to be a foolproof tool in accomplishing both of these tasks. By making a conscious commitment to follow them, you won't be able to—in fact won't *want* to—hide behind your prejudices and fears. The effect of these steps is to lift tension by offering the protection of a structured and reliable technique. The result is that you'll not only understand your partner better but also feel a kind of ease around each other, something you may have never experienced before, enabling you to hear and understand each other with unprecedented clarity.

You'll be helped to take full advantage of the steps by doing some preliminary work—not on your partner, but on yourself. What does this mean? Let's find out right now.

Preliminaries

START WITH "ME," NOT "WE"

LET'S FORGET ABOUT your "other half" for the moment and concentrate on you. Learning how to hear and be heard by the one you love depends first and crucially on achieving some clarity about your *own* feelings, fears, and defense mechanisms.

Why is this so important?

If what you want to do is communicate—to hear and speak to your partner with as much clarity, honesty, and satisfaction as possible—you need to learn about your own style of communication, what motivates you to feel and say what you do, what *you* are bringing to the equation. Why? Because when you understand more about how and why you react the way you do, you'll respond to your partner with more of your conscious self and less by reflex. Acting reflexively means relinquishing control over your own reactions and behavior. Put the simplest way, the more clearly you see yourself, the more truly you will be able to hear, understand, and accept other people.

So I want you to do something in these first pages and in the first two steps of this program: I want you to be selfish. Concentrate on your own feelings; for the moment, keep your partner out of it.

The mirror that I'll ask you to hold up will reveal your loves and hates, what you judge to be "good" and "bad," and will allow you to see more clearly why you have the assumptions and make the judgments you do. An important dividend of this is facing your own urge to blame something or someone outside yourself as the problem. We're not interested now in who is right or wrong—only in taking note of when and why you do affix blame. Be assured that you don't have to do or fix anything right now. All you have to do is take a *look* at yourself. The exercise in this chapter demonstrates one technique to help you step back from your life in order to observe some of the assumptions that determine the judgments you make. You'll come to see that you can *choose* the way you feel and behave. You'll begin to uncover and understand some of the less apparent reasons you "hate" certain things about your partner, and why you feel the urge to shut down or lash out.

But that's later on. Right now, making *any* progress in seeing yourself more clearly, holding up a mirror to your motivations and your defenses, is reason to celebrate. It's hard to look at our own defense mechanisms, most particularly the defensive reflex to blame or judge someone else. We have depended on these self-protective tactics to save us for so long that even the idea of questioning them can be uncomfortable, even frightening. But we do need to question them, because the fears that fuel our defenses are so crippling. Facing these fears is a simple, learnable process that I'll cover in later chapters. Our goal right now is simply to make you more aware of what motivates you to "hate" or "love" the things you do: just to see it. This will help you to feel safe enough to listen and speak—understanding that the aim of listening or speaking to your partner isn't to guard against attack, but to receive understanding.

The Connection Between Shame and Blame

Why is the prospect of intimacy so frightening?

Intimacy is a willingness to share, with someone you love and trust, areas of yourself where you feel shame or guilt or embarrassment. Unfortunately, the childhood roots of shame run deep and are usually so humiliating that even the suggestion of exploring them makes us freeze. And, commonly, when someone close to us gets too near these areas, we become defensive. We lash out or withdraw. We protect ourselves. Out of this defensiveness, we blame.

We've talked about how damaging blame can be in a general way. But what exactly are we doing when we blame?

The reflex to blame means looking outside ourselves for a villain instead of within to see what our own complicity is in what's going on, and it constitutes one of the biggest obstacles to intimate communication. Achieving intimacy is a process of facing, and ultimately getting beyond, this urge to blame by detoxifying your reactions to those parts of yourself you've labeled shameful. This is accomplished by putting feelings into words in the context of a relationship that feels safe, nonthreatening. Attempting this task with someone you trust can lead you, slowly, to become more accepting of yourself and consequently more emotionally available to your partner. In fact, as you begin to hear and speak to your partner in this context of safety, you simultaneously begin to hear and speak to *yourself* more honestly. Accomplishing this requires facing and discarding certain reflexive defenses, but it doesn't mean judging yourself (or anyone else) harshly—which, unfortunately, is what often happens when we get near our own shame.

To gain freedom from the constriction of shameful feelings, we need to uncover the defensive mechanisms that no longer work for us, to learn how these maneuvers distort our perceptions of our partners' behavior. This exploration requires a special kind of mental finesse and alertness, because we're dealing with *their* defensiveness as well as our own. Too often we descend into a tug-of-war from which there's no exit: "It's your fault. . . ." "No, it's your fault. . . ." "I wouldn't have done this if you hadn't done that, . . ." etc. However, when you can recognize your own defensive style, you're usually able to see those same self-defense mechanisms at work in your partner, too. You can understand, even empathize with, your partner in a new way.

You can begin to explore your own defenses more deeply by employing an amazingly effective technique I suggest to my clients, one that has enabled them to face their urge to blame, and to understand more of what goes on when they feel that urge. It's useful preliminary work: it can create an especially productive mental climate in which to approach the Seven Steps to Intimate Communication.

Becoming a Playwright

"Becoming a playwright" is a technique whereby I invite a client to put his or her life on a stage and then step down into the audience with me. I then ask the person to imagine being a playwright, the person who has written the scene and created the protagonist up on the stage. I ask if he or she is willing to write a new part for the star of the play (him- or herself), to see how the supporting characters might respond now that the star is feeding them different lines. Knowing that they can *choose* new words and behavior and "parts" invariably frees them from a doomed sense of fate or inevitability.

The point of this exercise is to demonstrate that we often get into a rut in the way we think about certain people and circumstances in our lives. Imagining your life as a play that you write and star in is a way of turning the prism on whatever rut you may be in: you give yourself the opportunity to see the "play" from different vantage points. You begin to see that, by changing the script—the star's lines, for example—you can create new outcomes. This gives you a sense of power—the power to change things. A dividend is that when you feel this power, you feel less defensive and thus less of an urge to blame other people. There's more space, more freedom in your attitude. You're not so quick to seek fault when you begin to feel power.

How does this work? Let's look at one couple who've learned to use the "Becoming a Playwright" technique.

Julia and Mark, both in their early thirties, came to me first for couple counseling. Julia is a lawyer who manages the legal department of a major insurance company. She is a beautiful woman, intelligent and competent, as well as rather cool and reserved. According to Mark, however, she was not only cool—she was icy. As talkative and extroverted as Julia was quiet and restrained, Mark summed up his wife: "You want to know what Julia has been like with me ever since we got married? A cold fish. I can't remember the last time she spoke to me as if she *liked* me, much less wanted to make love to me. And now I find out she's had an affair. The blunt truth is, she cheated on me, and I can't forgive her for it."

Julia sighed. "I'm so sick of this. It's always *my* fault. You know I wouldn't have done anything with another man if you hadn't already turned your back on me. Why don't you talk about some of the reasons I might have turned off to you? Like what you're doing with your colleague Ann?"

Mark was angry. "How many times do we have to go over this?" He turned to address me: "She's convinced I'm having an affair, and I'm not. What I *do* sometimes say is that I'm getting more warmth and attention from my associate than I've ever gotten from my wife, before *or* after her fling with this guy in Chicago. Classic case of wife goes on business trip and stays later than the conference. Now she's just trying to get back at me because she feels guilty. Accusing me of having an affair with Ann. She can't face up to what *she* did, that's what's really going on. So she's trying to trump up charges against me."

Julia dismissed him: "Oh, come on. Stop playing the innocent victim. You're a classic womanizer. You flirt with everybody—you always have. Why don't you talk about all the other extramarital affairs you've had? Don't you remember how *we* met?"

It turned out that Julia and Mark met while Mark was married to another woman, and began an extramarital affair that lasted for two years before Mark finally got divorced. They'd met as colleagues at the office shortly before Julia was offered a new job at a different company, which she took so as not to mix her business life with Mark. But she had, she said, "firsthand experience of how duplicitous Mark can be, of how he can act the innocent sinned-against husband and be carrying on a torrid affair in secrecy. I'm onto that game," she said, turning to Mark once again. "How could I not be? You played it with me—with me in Ann's role. The real truth is, you're glad I had that weeklong affair. It gave you an excuse to withdraw from me and turn to Ann!"

Julia didn't deny having the affair she'd had. "I was under tremendous pressure. Mark had railed against me for months, calling me a sexual zombie because I wasn't raging to go to bed with him every minute. I had an unbelievable caseload at work and I just couldn't be the perfect lover to him. He was like a little baby, throwing tantrums because he couldn't always get what he wanted. I also think he was jealous of my having gotten promoted to head of my department. It's the classic emasculation thing: he couldn't stand my having surpassed him in my career. And so he was even more angry, carping at everything I did. I'd never felt so alone when I went on that business trip to Chicago. And this guy Charles, whom I'd known for several months through work, got me at a vulnerable moment. I just needed some kindness and understanding from somebody. And maybe to prove to myself that I wasn't the sexual zombie Mark kept calling me. I don't know. I *am* sorry for it now. Because, for all that's happened, I want to try to make my marriage work. But Mark is making it impossible. In every way he knows how.''

It was an effort for Mark to keep quiet as Julia spoke. Finally he exploded. "Look—*she*'s the one who had the affair. I'm not the one making things impossible. I didn't go away on a business trip and go to bed with some stranger. I'm sorry, but it'll take more than a feeble apology to take away the damage she's done.''

Mark and Julia were at a standoff and neither would budge. I realized that before they could begin to hear and speak to each other without lashing out or withdrawing, they needed to do some work on themselves individually. They had to set the stage so that they were equipped, truly, to *listen* to each other. I began to see each of them separately, to help them become aware of the script each was writing so that they could begin to extricate themselves from the repetitive patterns that trapped them right now.

Julia's Script: What Goes Around Comes Around

I asked Julia when I first saw her alone to do the playwright exercise with me. For the moment, I wanted her to detach from her life, to come into the audience as the playwright and director to observe "Julia" on stage, the star who interacted with the supporting character "Mark." I asked her to talk about herself and Mark in the third person.

First, some character description: Who was "Julia," really? What was she like?

Julia paused for a moment, then said one word. "Trapped."

"Trapped by what?" I asked.

"By . . . expectations," she said slowly. "Julia has a secret," she finally admitted. "She wants to be *free*. When she first met Mark, it was incredible for both of them. I guess they were both protected by the fact that Mark was already married. It just made things more sexy, fun. We—sorry, *they*—were free, in a funny way. It was like kids playing hooky from school. They were doing something taboo, living on the edge. It was so exciting." She stopped for a moment and frowned. "It was Mark who kept saying that he wanted to get divorced and marry Julia. Julia thought that was a lovely thing to say, but, to tell you the truth, she never imagined what it would really be like if Mark *were* free to marry her. When finally he did get a divorce, it scared her."

"Why was Julia afraid?" I asked.

"Married men aren't supposed to leave their wives," Julia said carefully, as if reciting from some text she'd memorized. "I—'Julia,' that is—was shocked. She'd learned from her parents that however unhappy you got, whatever you did to hurt your spouse, you never left that spouse. You were married forever. And I guess privately Julia counted on Mark staying married—so that Julia could keep the free feeling she felt with Mark, the secret, taboo, exciting part, the free spirit way she felt when they made love passionately in rented rooms or after work behind the locked doors of an office. Suddenly, when they were free to marry, Julia began to shut down. She wasn't really prepared for this part. It was frightening to her. Plus she felt guilty. She'd broken up a marriage. Marriages weren't supposed to break up."

This, Julia decided, was the end of Act One of the play. Her title for it? "Married Men Never Leave Their Wives."

But what about Act Two? What happened after Julia and Mark got married? "Julia was unhappy," she said. "She'd taken away another woman's husband. She even felt guilty telling her parents she was getting married, despite the fact that they'd been pushing her to settle down with someone for a long time. She'd never told them about Mark—she wouldn't have dared to tell them that she'd had an affair with a married man—and so they were surprised to hear in the same breath not only Mark's name for the first time, but that she was getting married to him. It took a while to convince them she wasn't getting married because she was pregnant.

"Julia felt guilty about the whole beginning of the marriage. And it's true, she did shut down. Suddenly sex wasn't so great anymore. The sparkle, the excitement, were diminished. The truth is"—Julia paused, as if surprised with this new idea—"she felt she had to be punished." Julia stopped for a moment, then said slowly, again with the tone of reciting from a text: "What goes around comes around. You have to pay for your sins. That's straight from my—from Julia's—mother. That's what she'd heard all her life. And so," Julia continued hesitantly, as if picking her way through a forest she'd never been in before, "Julia went about punishing herself, I guess. Withdrawing from Mark. Starting to dislike him for his lack of ambition, for the fact that his career wasn't keeping pace with hers. It was stronger than that. Julia despised Mark after she'd been promoted to head of her department. The *man* was supposed to succeed this way, not the woman. That idea came from Julia's mother, too."

Julia started to cry. "It's like nothing had gone the way it was *supposed* to. And somehow it was all Julia's fault. She had to be punished." Julia paused for a moment, wiped her eyes with a tissue, and then furrowed her brow, struck by a new thought. "It just occurred to me that Julia had that affair with Charles in Chicago because she wanted Mark to turn against her. It was what she deserved. She'd been a bad girl. Mark needed to know that—and punish her for it. She had to do something to *make* him punish her for it."

We agreed we'd reached the end of Act Two, which Julia titled "What Goes around Comes Around."

And now we were at the beginning of Act Three. Only this

act hadn't been written yet. Before it took shape, I wanted Julia to accept that she was *capable* of writing a new part for the "star." After she gave me the first two acts, and thought about their titles—"Married Men Never Leave Their Wives" and "What Goes Around Comes Around"—she could recognize these titles as old, entrenched assumptions that kept her thinking in a rut. Now, with Act Three ahead of her, she could choose to question those assumptions. She could choose to change habitual thinking, to learn that she didn't have to be bound by old messages she'd gotten from her parents, especially her mother.

Doing this meant accepting control and responsibility in crafting her own life. It meant not blaming anybody. It meant achieving clarity. Julia's task was to see her past actions as clearly as she could and to identify the assumptions from which she was operating—to see how or if they were holding her back.

She discovered not only her desire to be a free spirit, but also that she'd chosen Mark very carefully—that his personality enabled her to manipulate him in predictable ways. As she viewed the character "Mark" in her play, she saw that every time he felt rejected, he looked for someone else. While he may not have been having a sexual affair with Ann, he was certainly turning to Ann emotionally. Julia had succeeded in manipulating Mark to "cheat" on her. She knew that if she withdrew, Mark would turn to the nearest available sympathetic partner. By having the affair in Chicago, she clinched this. She made *sure* Mark would turn away from her. The bottom line: she could control Mark, make him punish her, by withdrawing her love.

And Mark, as he would discover when we explored his own play, was a slave to love. He was, Julia knew, impulsive. He was in fact very much the "baby" she had accused him of being. Julia knew that when he couldn't get immediate gratification from one source, he reflexively searched for another, and she used this knowledge as a tool. She knew she could manipulate him very easily with it.

But the main point is that Julia faced Act Three with much more information about herself and Mark than she'd had at the beginning of the play. What new act did she want to write, in light of these revelations?

As she thought about Act Three, Julia began to realize that if she truly didn't want to feel trapped, she had to free herself of the notion that she must be a certain way, play a certain role, and obey certain rigid requirements in order for her marriage to succeed. Accepting this was frightening at first. It meant Julia had to work without a net. She had to live in the moment. In choosing not to be a slave to the old assumptions that had always given shape to her world, she was opening herself to the Unknown.

Living in the moment means accepting that anything might happen. It also means that *what you do is important.* Suddenly you realize that you're the architect of your own life. But when all you know is what you're "supposed" to do, the real, conscious you isn't being consulted. You're not making who you really are, and what you really want, very important. Assumptions are directing and taking the place of your conscious choice-making self.

It's blind assumptions like these that were battling each other in Julia and Mark's marriage, not the conscious Julia and Mark. Understanding this gave Julia the title for her third act: "I Don't Have to Be a Certain Way." She knew now that writing a satisfying Act Three would have to be a continuous process of *choosing* what she wanted or didn't want to do, how she wanted to communicate with her husband, choosing on the basis of her real feelings, not a reflexive adherence to old, received assumptions. Yes, it might be scary, because it was traveling into the Unknown. But it gave her her only chance at freedom.

Mark's Script: I'd Never Join a Club That Would Let Me In

When Mark got the idea of the playwright game, that he could go down into the first row of the orchestra section and take notes on himself as an actor in a play, he described a very sorrowful scene. His description of the first act, covering his childhood, was relatively short, but sad, powerful, and telling: " 'Mark' always felt different from other people, especially from anyone in his family," he said. Mark was the only one who succeeded in school—nobody else in his family had. Mark came from what he called "a small-town, poor-white-trash family." He hated calling his family that, but he was sure that's how much of the rest of the world saw them. Certainly the rich and successful society to which he aspired would have mocked his uneducated and out-of-work father, his six brothers and sisters, and a mother who was never home because she had to clean other people's houses for a living.

Mark was driven to escape this dead-end world. But he always felt like an impostor. Sure, he learned to put on a good act. He was popular at the state university from which he received a scholarship—he was outgoing, good looking, quick witted—and he knew he was attractive to women. He knew he had considerable personal power. But deep down, it all felt like a sham. And as for love, well, he never truly trusted it. He'd never felt loved as a child, and the love of women that he attracted later in life felt false. They were loving an image he was projecting, not the real Mark.

So this was Act One. What might he title it? He made a suggestion: "I Have to Pretend to Be Someone Else to Be Accepted."

Act Two had to do with his relationships with women. He'd married twice before meeting Julia. His first wife was a college sweetheart whose father was a successful lawyer and who encouraged his son-in-law to become a lawyer, too. The marriage couldn't survive the pressures of law school—that was at least part of the public reason Mark gave for why it fell apart. But more deeply, Mark realized that his feelings of being an impostor attacked him and his feelings about his wife and her family. Whenever she gave even a hint of criticizing him, Mark overreacted. He was never good enough— that's what he was sure his wife and her family felt, and was sure they were saying behind his back. He began to notice other women law students, did his "adorable misunderstood husband act," and started an affair with one of them. When his wife found out, she demanded a divorce. Mark blamed his wife's constant criticism for making him turn to another woman. He never considered the possibility that he might have had a hand in his marriage's breakup. It was always, clearly, "her fault."

Mark got through law school, passed the bar exam after the second try, and got a job with reasonably good prospects at a major firm, but he was never as ravenously ambitious as a lot of his co-workers. He was always looking for "the right woman": that, he was sure, was the missing ingredient in his life. But now that he thought about how he met his second wife, Margery, he began to realize he was looking for someone to save him. He was looking for someone secure and loving and, he hoped, rich enough to make him feel safe. Margery fit the bill. She was several years older than Mark, she came from a prominent and very wealthy family, she had no money worries, and—on cue—she fell in love with Mark. But this second marriage turned out to be just as rocky as his first. Mark felt snubbed by Margery's parents; again he got the message that he "wasn't good enough." He began to feel kept by Margery, as if he were some kind of pet Margery turned to whenever she needed sex or affection. He became as ultrasensitive to her criticisms as he had been with his first wife. He felt trapped.

Then he met Julia. Mark's gaze grew distant for a moment

and he smiled. "Julia seemed so different from every other woman I'd—*'Mark'*—had met. She was so lively, so willing to do things on a dare, so quick." Although she was quiet, Mark sensed a fire in her, a real passion. And she didn't seem hung up on all the proprieties, the way Margery and her "highfalutin" family always were. She was refreshing. Mark fell in love with her and began an affair. It was conducted in the greatest secrecy, which Julia seemed to enjoy. The forbidden quality of it titillated her, he realized. But that same secrecy began to bother him. He didn't want to have this relationship in the dark. He wanted to marry Julia, live out in the open with her. And so he told his wife about his affair and that he wanted a divorce. Margery had already become disgusted with him and put up no resistance—she seemed eager to get rid of him. So he married Julia. "And things started, once again, to go downhill. . . ."

Mark sighed deeply. I asked him what he thought we should title this second act. He thought for a moment, then said: "I'm Always Yearning for Something I Can't Get." Then he frowned and shook his head. "No, it's something even more basic." He said, slowly: "I'd Never Join a Club That Would Let Me In," paraphrasing Groucho Marx. "How's that for a title?"

I thought it was interesting that Mark made this leap. I asked him to explain. "As I was telling you all this, I realized that every time I got what I thought I wanted, I didn't want it anymore. Why was that? Why did I turn on my first wife, then on Margery, and now on Julia? Well, I'm still not crazy that Julia had an affair. That still hurts more than I can say. I don't think I've begun to explore those feelings, really. But I see a big problem now, a problem in me. It's this damned feeling of inferiority. If somebody accepts me, then *they* can't be worth much, can they? Look at the worthless goods they accepted! I never realized before now that I was working from such low self-esteem."

This realization freed Mark to be able to approach his Act Three with more clarity, just as Julia's revelations began to clear the way for her own Act Three. The assumptions that Mark needed to question and give up had to do with his deep feeling of worthlessness, that he was an impostor, that anyone who loved him was deluded, either because they'd fallen for his act or because they themselves were lacking.

Only now were Mark and Julia truly ready to listen to each other. The insights they gained from being their own playwrights prepared them for the process of speaking and listening to each other. Because of what they've learned about themselves, that their motivations are more complicated and less conscious than they had realized, they are more disposed to be tolerant of each other. They have less urge to blame. This doesn't mean that ''Becoming a Playwright'' has solved everything. Mark is still wounded by Julia's affair. And he hasn't magically released all his old assumptions: his first reflex will still be to act as if he's not worth much. Julia's old assumptions haven't magically disappeared either. She needs to face them again as, inevitably, they'll continue to come up. What's important is that Mark and Julia have cleared the way to begin to hear each other.

The good news is, even when one partner allows him- or herself to become their own playwright—and even when one partner initiates the steps you'll start exploring in the rest of this book—*both* of you are ahead. Clarity on either of your parts will ultimately help both of you. Now that Julia realizes that many of her assumptions are what held her back from understanding both Mark and herself, she is more tolerant of Mark. She is in a position to benefit more easily and completely from the process of listening on which my seven-step program is based. It's the same with Mark. But even if Mark hadn't done this playwright exploration, the fact that *Julia* had would help both to forge ahead. At least she would be aware that she is free to choose how she thinks and feels, that she can override old assumptions and reflexive ways of thinking and responding.

Doing the Playwright Exercise Yourself

It might seem like the playwright exercise asks you to take on your whole life in one gulp. But truly, you don't have to create a lavish stage production to benefit from stepping off the stage and taking a look at the "play" of your life. Start with a small scene. Getting even the barest glimpse of what's going on in one episode of your life can be liberating. Keep the stakes small at first.

What scene should you start with?

Start with something specific but emotionally charged. You might begin with a childhood memory—an episode when you felt ashamed, "caught in the act," or one when you felt angry and victimized. Let's say you remember a parent blaming you for something your younger sister did. Take careful note of what your parent said, and how you defended yourself, how you *felt* at the time. Take note of any frustration—for example, "Dad still doesn't believe me even though I keep telling him I didn't do it"—and how being blamed made you feel. What did you say back to your father? How did his lack of trust make you feel?

Now, quickly, free-associate to a more recent episode in your life with your partner. You'll very likely focus on a similar feeling of frustration and powerlessness, but not necessarily. Whatever the free association brings, put it on stage and give each character a script. If it's a similar scene—your partner accusing you of something unjustly—take note of the way you feel, what you say to defend yourself. Perhaps the scene will reverse: you'll focus on an episode in which you rail against your partner for something you feel he did to hurt you. What exactly do you say to him? How do you attempt to persuade him that he did wrong? What does he say back? How does this make you feel?

What you'll discover are not only the "triggers" that upset you, but also the feelings, language, and behavior they trigger *in* you. Try to tolerate your feelings of distress, and maintain some distance from them. Remember that you're in the audience and that the characters up on stage are acting out a play. Don't become them: just observe them. You don't have to do anything about the play right now, you don't have to change anything. Our aim is simple and limited: to provide a mirror so that you can see that something *is* triggering the character playing you to react in certain ways. All I want you to do now is to realize that certain past experiences trigger your current reactions. This eventually will help you to understand why the character resorts to those reactions. Which, in turn, will give you, as the playwright, a greater sense of choice. The thought will occur to you that the main character, the actor playing *you,* can choose to speak and behave differently.

All we're doing is opening the door to choice. Stepping off the stage of your life for a moment, sitting in the audience, looking as dispassionately as you can at the characters in front of you, taking note of what they say, will help you to understand something about their motivations. What does the hero or heroine—"you"—believe? What are his or her assumptions? What creates anger or sorrow or relief?

Once you've experimented with a few scenes, you can begin to do what Mark and Julia did: make out the structure of the longer play. Your first childhood scene can expand to give you a first act, one for which you may be able to find an apt title. Let's stay with our example of having been treated unjustly by your father as a child. You might call this first act "The Victim."

Let's then think about what you might call the next episode involving you and your partner. You are now railing at your partner for doing something that hurt you very much. And he/she doesn't get it—won't give you so much as an apology. You get angrier, the volume rises, and ultimatums are given. Take note of what causes the escalation of anger between you. What words particularly cut, hurt? Out of this may come a title for the act. Perhaps "He'll Never Understand."

By this time, even with two small specific scenes, you'll have evidence of certain patterns, triggers, that have an inevitable result. He says something, you get angry. You say something, he gets angry. The "something" is important. These are the words, you see from the audience, that the characters are choosing to say, even if, until now, that choice has been unconscious. Now, as the result of listening carefully to each character, you see that the words spoken are *chosen.*

That's all I want you to see right now. That there is choice involved in how each of you speaks and behaves toward the other.

As a result of deciphering the acts of their own plays, Mark and Julia made two general discoveries, which I expect you will make, too:

1. Many of our old assumptions trap us and rob us of choice.
2. We have much more power over our lives than we realized we had.

As you saw with Julia, the power you discover is sometimes frightening. We don't cling to our old assumptions for no reason. They give, as Julia put it, "shape" to our lives: they give us order, they tell us what to do, what things "ought" to be like. They seem to give us clear grounds for blaming anyone who does not behave according to their dictates. But they also block the possibility of real communication. As George Bernard Shaw paraphrased Socrates: "A life unexamined is not worth living." The playwright exercise allows you simultaneously to live in the moment while observing what you are doing.

Understanding more about the nature of blame—why we do it and how we can begin to resist the urge—is, in fact, very important groundwork for getting the most out of the rest of this book. You'll profit most when you approach your love partner with some knowledge of who *you* are, as the playwright exercise will help you to do. When you can overcome or at least question the urge to blame your partner, you're ready to explore the process of intimate listening outlined in the following pages.

The Seven Steps to Intimate Communication

Now Julia and Mark are at the brink of even larger discoveries. They're ready to hear each other in some unanticipated ways. What are the steps that will help them to do this? Here they are in their bare form:

1. **Recognizing tension**
2. **Crossing the street**
3. **Engaging the outer ear**
4. **Activating the inner ear**
5. **Reaching for the past**
6. **Empathizing through detachment**
7. **Building a bridge**

Exploring these steps is the task of the rest of this book. But before you learn what each of these steps means and how to make use of each one, a word of reassurance—even a guarantee:

There isn't one couple I've worked with who haven't been able to benefit from these steps, even if (as you'll discover from time to time) you may not always be able to get past the first or second step. (As you'll learn, sometimes simply "recognizing tension" and "crossing the street" are sufficient to give you the necessary distance and clarity to see what's going on between you.) Another important premise and promise: you get this whole process rolling *yourself*—by listening. Certainly the ideal is to have your partner learn from the steps how to listen to you as well, so you both can learn more deeply what feelings of anger, frustration, fear, or sadness are blocking you. But even when only one partner is capable of employing these "intimate listening" steps, both partners usually benefit.

Remember that the goal here is to *hear* your partner, not to change his or her behavior. (The decision whether or not to do something different has to come from the speaker himself, a process that comes *after* these steps, when he has more understanding of what motivates his behavior, not during them). The goal is to understand that behavior—in other words, to *communicate*. This happens as the speaker gains more self-knowledge, and the listener gains more empathy. At the very least, the listening partner develops a new clarity and even, usually, a new feeling of peace and acceptance of her partner. She may also be able to use some of the feedback she receives (when her partner tells her what's bothering him) to change her own behavior.

Not every couple stays together as a result of following these steps. Sometimes the clarity this process makes possible reveals that both partners are at a genuine stalemate: they may see that their agendas or desires are basically at odds, and they may decide, as a result, that the relationship simply can't work. But in my experience, most couples who learn to hear each other according to these guidelines discover whole new areas in which they can *connect*—understand and empathize and nurture each other more completely and creatively. Their relationships become better: more loving, more accepting, more satisfying.

The isolation of thinking you'll never be able to understand or be understood by the person you love can be one of the most deeply painful experiences of our lives. Luckily, we have the power to create a route to that understanding. There are steps we can take to allow one soul to reach another. Perhaps that's the most important goal here: to show how one person can allow another person's soul to emerge, to be seen, accepted, loved.

A Word About Doing the Steps

As you begin the adventure of this seven-step process, be patient: this isn't a program anyone expects you to do perfectly or quickly. I suggest that you simply read through the whole book right now, getting an overall picture of the process that the steps describe so that you have some idea where you're going before you actually start the process with your partner. Let yourself be a beginner: read, first only with the goal of becoming familiar with these ideas, to get a view of the larger picture.

Then, go back to Steps One and Two, "Recognizing Tension" and "Crossing the Street," which don't involve anyone but you. Try to follow their suggestions, which, as you'll see, are designed to give you meditative "space." Experiment with these two steps (you'll see that you can do them without your partner even knowing it) to give yourself the experience of detaching, removing yourself from the "storm."

You'll now be ready to venture into the remaining steps. An important virtue of this process is that you get it going simply by *listening*. Your partner doesn't have to agree to "play." Also, there are no timetables: you will find that you'll do as many steps as you need to do, as you and your partner are emotionally ready to do. After a while, you won't be conscious that you're doing "Step Two" or "Step Five"—you'll see the whole arc as something organic, something you do, and want to do, naturally.

What about getting your partner to learn these steps and apply them, listening to *you?* What if he or she resists the idea of following ''steps,'' or undergoing what may seem like an artificial ''self-help'' program? First of all, don't try to ''get'' your partner to do anything. Coercion never works. What I can virtually guarantee, however, is that the expanded consciousness and feeling of ease you enjoy as the result of listening according to these steps will turn out to be contagious. You will have created a softer, more receptive environment for both people, an atmosphere that will seduce your partner into a greater receptivity to *you.* Don't be surprised if he or she asks you, ''What's that book you've been reading?'' But even if your spouse doesn't reach for this book, the fact that you are following these steps will only help to increase clarity and good will between the two of you.

The main point is to be patient with both yourself and your partner. Immerse yourself in these steps as gradually as you need to. You'll find benefits at every point in your journey; there are no time requirements for when to do, or how long to spend doing, any of these steps. The rewards, I promise you, will be self-evident.

STEP ONE

RECOGNIZING TENSION

STEP ONE, "RECOGNIZING TENSION," means sensitizing yourself to moments when you experience stress or tension.

The value of recognizing tension in yourself is that it wakes you up: you realize that it's time to shift gears and listen to your partner differently. The ways you express tension may be as obvious as yelling, throwing (or wanting to throw) a lamp at someone, or otherwise exploding in a sudden angry outburst. Generally, however, they're a lot more subtle: jangling coins in your pocket; suddenly becoming silent; even assuming a guise of serenity or cheerfulness.

Remember, we're still talking about *you*, not your partner. As you've seen from our preliminaries, you have to start by increasing awareness that certain triggers cause you to choose to react in a certain way. Recognizing your own tension really means recognizing that something in the moment is causing you to feel stress—something has just happened to activate the reflex to tense up.

This may not seem like a big deal. You may be thinking, "It's no secret when I get tense! I know when the volume of my voice rises, when I feel like throwing a frying pan at somebody. Why devote so much time to that?" Actually, many of the ways we become tense aren't obvious at all. They can be very subtle. You may be so used to employing them that you have little or no idea you're doing it.

For some vivid illustration of this, let's look at how Julia and Mark learned to see how they each expressed tension. Then, more briefly, we'll explore a number of ways others have discovered that they betray their tension. Finally, we'll extract from their experience guidelines you can use to uncover your own tension tactics. There's more to discover here than you may think.

Silence as a Sign of Tension: Julia

Shortly before Julia and Mark came to see me, they had bought their first house together. "Partly I think we did it for the same reason some couples decide to have a baby. We thought it would bring us closer together," Julia said. "But I also wanted a home to work on. I've always had this ideal of a dream home; now it seemed like we could turn it into reality." They bought a medium-size late-Victorian house in suburban Long Island that needed a lot of work. Julia had always known generally that she resented Mark for not being as gung ho about working on the house as she was. But she was amazed as she began to realize just how deep this resentment ran, what it was connected to in her childhood and the ways in which it provoked her to express tension.

Typically, when Julia talked about working on the house on the weekends, she began with a long, deep sigh, as if nobody could possibly understand how overwhelming it was. A perfectionist, Julia wanted to do a lot of the sanding, plastering, painting, and wallpapering herself. She didn't trust the average contractor to carry out her detailed plans; plus it saved money to do it alone. She said she felt she was "attacking" the house every weekend. "I'll get up about six-thirty on a Saturday morning, make coffee, and draw out my battle plans of what needs to be done that day. Then I'll sand or paint furiously for hours at a time. Mark helps, too, after he gets up much later in the morning—closer to noon—but I can tell his heart isn't in it. I didn't know how much this bothered me until recently."

I asked Julia to recall and describe her feelings right before she launched into the weekend's work. What emotional adjectives would she use to describe how she felt before she picked up the paintbrush? At first Julia looked at me as if I were crazy: wasn't it self-evident? "I want to get the job done!" she said, as if that explained everything. But that, I said, wasn't really answering the question. What *feelings* came up about "getting the job done"?

Julia paused for a moment, then began, slowly, to describe emotions to which she clearly hadn't given much attention before. "I feel driven," she said. "More than driven—pushed by something inside me, something so strong that it's almost scary. It's like if I don't do what's on my list, don't do it perfectly, I'll be punished for it. I don't know who I think is going to punish me, but that's the feeling. I'm also angry. I'm angry at Mark for not helping me, for not being as anxious about the work as I am. It seems like he's not only uninterested in the house but he doesn't care much about me either."

Julia began to see that "attacking" the house the way she did every weekend had a useful function for her. It pushed down some frightening and uncomfortable feelings. She dealt with these deeper anxieties by throwing herself into furious work. "Attacking" was exactly the right word for what she did. She was fighting back feelings she was afraid might overwhelm her if she wasn't vigilant in controlling and burying them. One fortunate dividend is that she was indeed getting a lot of work done on the house. But a less fortunate dividend, she began to see, is that the emotions she was striving so assiduously (if up until now less than consciously) to bury weren't getting buried deeply enough. They kept hissing up in other ways. As belligerent as she sometimes was with Mark in couple counseling (railing at Mark for his unforgiving nature, etc.), she realized that a much more frequent tactic she employed with him was simply to shut down. When Mark would enter the torn-up living room in the middle of the day—a living room Julia had already been working on for hours—Julia would barely more than nod a greeting at him. She was silent. It was how, she realized, she generally dealt with him—how she expressed her tension at his presence. It had never occurred to her that that's what she was doing. "I always just thought I was wrapped up in the work," she said. "But I guess more was going on."

As she stayed with these feelings, allowed herself to remember, and, in memory, experience the tension that Mark made her feel simply by walking into the room, certain childhood recollections began to filter through. This is very common. When you allow yourself to experience the impact of your feelings, they often come attached to other feelings and memories. Much more is submerged than we ever bargain for.

"Being silent," Julia said, "was something my family always did whenever there was conflict. It's like nobody ever wanted to notice when anything was wrong. Most of the time, we all struggled like crazy to make sure that nothing *went* wrong. I remember when I was a little girl—I couldn't have been older than four or five—it was early evening, it had just gotten dark, and I was too afraid to go up the stairs to the bathroom. Nobody had turned on the light. I was mortified. Mommy and Daddy were out on the back porch having coffee after dinner, a time when it was clear I wasn't supposed to bother them. But I had to go to the bathroom so badly. I was afraid to call out to them, but even more afraid to go up the stairs myself. So I peed in my pants. I remember today how embarrassing it was to feel all wet, to know I was messing up the rug in the living room. I started to cry. Just then, my father walked in. He saw what had happened. He didn't scold me. He didn't say anything. He went into the kitchen to get some towels, wiped my legs and the rug, and without a word took me up to the bathroom so he could clean me up more thoroughly. I still remember how coldly he went through all these motions, saying nothing. Finally he did say, 'You're old enough to go upstairs and turn on the light. I don't want this to happen again.' And that was it. No more mention was ever made of it.''

Julia had always thought of her upbringing as what she called "classic repressed WASP." But this was a term she used dismissively; she'd never really given it much thought beyond this. She had never truly allowed herself to *feel* what it meant to be that terrified little girl so many years ago, wanting to pee, being so afraid to call out to her parents. Indeed, she had learned to see silence and the self-sufficiency it signified as evidence of virtue. "If you want to get something done, do it yourself" was one of her most frequently repeated mottos. "Stop whining" was another. All the terror and anger she'd felt as a little girl was clamped down upon, not allowed expression, shoved behind the lessons her parents taught her about "doing it yourself" and "getting it right." Her repressed feelings still had enormous energy, however: they fueled her perfectionism, her drive to get things done quickly and well, even today. But they had never been allowed to come up as what they were: terror and anger.

Then Julia thought back to her college days, when she had, she remembered, tried to rebel a bit. "The first time I went to a frat party," she says, "I got terribly drunk. I *loved* the feeling. It was like, for the first time in my life, all of my inhibitions just flew away. I felt free, seductive, funny—like some animal, pent up in a cage all its life, had been finally let out. But it was scary, too. The message I'd gotten from my family was always 'Be normal. Stay in control. You can't get what you want if you don't work at it.' In high school I guess I was what you'd call an overachiever, a cheerleader, yearbook editor, on the student council, honor society, the whole bit. Life seemed like something you had to spend every minute juggling so everything would get done at once, and perfectly—

but you couldn't let anyone see that you were sweating. You not only had to do everything, you had to do it gracefully. So getting drunk was wonderful, because it gave me the feeling I could just *stop* all my frantic maneuvering." Julia groaned softly, remembering: "But the next day—of course the hangover didn't help—I felt all this terrible guilt. What had I done, said, the night before? Not being able to remember anything scared the hell out of me. It meant admitting that, for an evening, I'd actually allowed myself to lose control."

Julia said that this began a history in college of bouncing back and forth between drunken frat parties and dates and then swearing she'd never do it again, becoming the perfectly self-controlled student she knew she was supposed to be, until the tension got so great that she got drunk again. "I finally stopped after one night when I drove myself home drunk and nearly killed myself by crashing into a tree. I made a vow not to drink too much after that, a vow I've kept."

But Julia's feelings kept erupting nonetheless. "That's when I started having affairs with married men," she says. "Which brings us to Mark—remember, I started with him while he was still married. It was the forbidden part that turned me on." Actually being in a marriage, Julia realized, felt like she had to return to being the Best Little Girl in the World. And what that Best Little Girl did when she felt tense was, typically, to shut down, be silent, show no emotion.

Julia had never recognized this before. But now she knows that if she looks into a mirror and sees a face showing no emotion, she's in a state of tension. In fact, the higher she functions—the better she is at juggling all the details of her life—the greater her tension is. "It's ironic," she says now. "I used to think this self-control meant I was serene. That I wasn't allowing myself to be bothered by anything. Now it turns out that this 'serenity' is really masking a lot of tension."

So, for Julia, recognizing tension in herself meant catching herself being silent. Silence, for Julia, turned out not to be so silent after all.

Calming the Whirling Dervish: Mark

Mark faces some very different challenges in being able to recognize his tension. When I articulated this first step to him, he shrugged it off, as if it were the simplest thing in the world. "You want to know when I'm tense? I'll tell you. I always know how I feel and I've never been shy about telling anyone else. I don't understand these WASP types, like Julia, who hold it all in. I've never held anything in. When I'm angry, I blow up. When I'm sad, I cry. When I'm happy, I laugh. What's the big deal?"

And indeed, Mark had learned to deal with and express his feelings very differently from Julia. His problem was that in his frequent emotional explosions, he was actually blocking contact with himself, acting out in furious, hysterical, whirling-dervish style the least feeling, especially any feeling that caused him discomfort—getting it *out* of him so that he wouldn't have to face and feel it. Yes, he was "open," but his constant state of emotional outpouring meant that he was never able to understand much about what he kept letting out.

Mark felt himself to be the most honest person in the world. However, true honesty doesn't mean spilling out everything you think and feel indiscriminately. In his zeal to let the world know how he was feeling, Mark rarely took time to reflect on his feelings or understand where they were coming from and how they affected the rest of his life. He was, in fact, as afraid of facing his feelings as Julia was afraid to face hers. They simply got rid of them in different ways. He spewed them; Julia buried them.

Spewing and burying each have their payoffs. When you "throw up" your feelings, you often do experience a momentary relief. Burying feelings can enable you, at least in the short run, to function better in day-to-day life—as Julia put it, "to get things done right." However, each has its downside. As we saw with Julia, burying feelings can create such subterranean tension that from time to time you're likely to erupt, go completely out of control, and sabotage everything you've worked to build. Tightly controlled people typically "blow" in very self-destructive ways. Similarly, spewing out your feelings without reflecting on their meaning and their impact keeps you in a rut. Mark could never learn anything about himself while he was in a state of "gushing." While Julia benefited from learning that she could let the reins go a bit, Mark had to be encouraged to pull back on them.

In fact, Mark's challenge was in some ways greater than Julia's. When Julia realized how much her silence hid, she learned a clear lesson. Silence, for her, was a sign that she was holding something back. It made sense to her, given her awareness of how she had learned to repress her feelings throughout her life, that something *was* being held back, something it could profit her to look at. However, it took Mark a long while to realize that "expressing" his feelings the way he did wasn't a means of understanding them; in fact, his behavior was blocking a more reflective and deeper contact with himself.

What helped Mark was recognizing the behavior patterns he'd learned from his family. You'll remember that he felt ashamed of his poor and underachieving family. He was the first one to go to college, the first one to "make it" in the wider world. But as much as he wanted to sever himself from his family, he'd been marked by his childhood in some irrevocable ways. In search of work, or simply because they couldn't pay the rent or mortgage on whatever home they'd managed to move into, Mark's family kept moving. "There was always a lot of high drama about it," he said. "Dad would come home, usually drunk, and explode about his mistreatment at the job he'd just been fired from, and what we all really needed was a fresh start. So we'd pack up, sometimes at night, and move somewhere else. This happened eight, maybe ten times between first grade and when I graduated high school. I never had the same group of friends for longer than two years. I was always pulling up and having to establish myself in a new school. It was horrible. I was always the misfit. The only lesson I got out of all this was: Hit the ground running. Keep moving. It's like they kept on dropping me into new battlefields and I was always at war. Make a lot of noise, establish your territory, be just plain louder than the next guy. That was how you got your way.''

Mark began to realize that his continual ''self-expression'' was in fact a chronic running away from his feelings. ''Get them out before they hurt you'' was his motto about emotions. Typically, when he'd get up, walk into the living room, and see his silent wife grimly working away at the walls, he'd rush into a harangue: ''Why are you working so hard? Why don't we hire some professionals to do this stuff? Why are you trying to run everything all the time?'' His anger and frustration were evident.

What Mark needed to learn was that he could survive the feeling of tension without running away from it. Recognizing tension for him meant slowing down, choosing silence for a moment, allowing his feelings to ''be,'' so that he wasn't off and running away from them and acting or speaking reflexively.

Mark and Julia made some surprising discoveries about the way they experienced and expressed tension. Julia saw that her supposedly serene shutting down wasn't so serene after all; in fact it was a strong signal that she had put up her defenses and was very much in a state of tension. Mark discovered that he never allowed himself to *tolerate* tension for long enough to recognize it. Recognizing tension means, for Mark, allowing it to *be* for the moment, not fleeing it. But for both

Mark and Julia, recognizing tension has meant some substantial revelations. It wasn't as simple as they'd once thought.

Categorizing Your Tension Tactics

There are numerous other behaviors that we may not immediately recognize as ways of expressing tension. Here are six general personality categories and the obstacles to recognizing tension these personalities often face. These by no means exhaust the range of resistances people commonly bring to Step One, but they should nonetheless enlighten you about many of your own (often hidden) tension tactics.

The Somatizer. "Honey, I'd love to talk to you about this but I have such a headache I can hardly see." "I can't deal with anything right now with this terrible cold." "You know how my arthritis acts up when the humidity changes. . . ." Somatizing means channeling your feelings into physical ailments. It's not that many aches and illnesses aren't real, but for some people, they become signs of tension—that uncomfortable feelings are being buried. This is typically the case with such stress-related illnesses as rheumatoid arthritis, migraine headaches, and colitis. As much purely physical basis as there may be for these illnesses, there is often a significant emotional trigger or component as well.

But that emotional part can be difficult to face up to. A woman I know took great offense when I suggested that her migraines might have some connection to her feelings about her husband. She lashed out: "You think I *want* these migraines? You think they're imaginary, like I'm putting them on? You should have one yourself, then you'd know what hell they are. . . ." It is frightening to take responsibility for somatizing; to admit that perhaps your emotional state *does* have something to do with why you're ill. As with every other defense you've learned, you probably can't imagine existing without it. However, remember that all we're doing right now is focusing on awareness of this. Admitting that a headache or a cold may be signs of a stressed-out immune system is simply that: admitting it. That's all this first step is about.

The Overly Cheery. This is another slippery sign of tension. It's not always clear when cheerfulness is forced. We may have learned so deeply to "look on the bright side" that we haven't a clue that our sunny views are covering something darker. Our subsequent behavior may, however, give us a clue. People who insist that everything is fine, who have complete faith that it will all turn out for the best, who count their blessings every day, yet who sabotage their best efforts at achieving their goals, are covering tension and anxiety with cheeriness and self-destructive acting-out (for someone trying to lose weight, for example, it could be reaching for that second piece of chocolate cake).

Our tensions *will* out, somehow. If you know that you resort to cheerfulness as a cover-up, then you've located one of your signs of tension. Again, all I'm asking you to do is recognize the possibility.

The Perfectionist. Julia realized that part of her obsession with painting the living-room wall was with "doing it right." She was driven by a fierce perfectionism. Compulsive attention to detail marks the perfectionist, but admitting this isn't always easy. Perfectionists often resort to "getting things right" so reflexively and unconsciously that they're unaware of the tension it's causing them.

The list of the perfectionist's compulsions is endless. It can range from addictive or obsessive/compulsive disorders such as automatically reaching for a drink or a drug when you feel discomfort, or returning three times to your apartment to make *really* sure one last time that the lights are all out, to any number of forms of perfectionism: folding toilet paper in a certain way, straightening out your socks so that they're color-coordinated, and so on. Superstitiously adhering to ritual behavior—for example, "Step on a crack, you'll break your mother's back"—is another common perfectionist (and obsessive/compulsive) tactic. It might be as simple as doodling while you're on the phone, noticing that you're pressing down hard with the pencil, or obsessing over creating a precise geometric pattern.

Our purpose here, once again, isn't to criticize this behavior but merely to suggest that it might be another sign of tension for you.

The Blamer. We've already spent some time investigating how distracting and damaging blame can be. But we can now meet it head-on as a prime sign that you're feeling tension. This is another slippery one, however. As with somatizing, which involves blaming how we feel on physical pain or illness, other forms of blaming or finding scapegoats are very effective and often very reflexive ways of masking and getting rid of tension. We may have a lot invested in our scapegoats and be very unwilling to see them as evasions of responsibility.

Blaming means taking the focus off yourself. If it's always somebody else's fault, you're off the hook. You may deny that you have any choice *but* to blame: "If you were in my place, you'd feel the same way!" Certainly you may be facing and battling some real injustice. However, when you feel the urge to blame all of your problems on an outside villain (whether it's the IRS or your mother-in-law), you've found another wake-up signal: it's likely that something more is going on here than simple victimization. At the very least, you've found a sign that tension is probably sky-high. All systems are on "Defend." And that, again, is all we're interested in noticing at the moment.

The Advice-Giver. The urge to "fix" other people can sometimes be overwhelming. What it also can be is a sign that you're tense. It's interesting to note that the motive behind giving advice often has more to do with making *you* feel better than it does making whomever you're talking to feel better. Anyone who's spent time sick in the hospital probably has tales of visitors who talk about nothing but what the patient should do—what he should eat, what he should make his doctor do, how he should change his lifestyle so he won't get sick again. Whether this advice is good or bad is irrelevant. The point is that the advice-giver is usually trying to allay his own anxiety—to get rid of the problem so *he*'ll feel better. It's often the same with the advice you may feel impelled to give your partner. If you're honest about the motive, you almost always discover that what you're trying to do is rid yourself of the anxiety of being in the presence of a problem. You want to fix things so they'll go away.

But our aim here is simply to point out that when you feel the urge to rush in and fix somebody else, you've found a prime tension signal.

The Moralist. Every time you stand in judgment of someone else, you're expressing tension. This is as slippery as any of the signals we've explored, because, once again, you probably have a lot invested in the morality behind your judgments. If you feel that someone is doing something obviously wrong, you can't help judging him. We're not concerned with the rightness or wrongness of anyone else's behavior right now, however. All we're concerned with is awakening you to the tension that the urge to judge both reflects and provokes in you. Once again, all you have to do is notice this, not change it.

Undoubtedly, one or more of the preceding categories of tension signals have rung a bell for you. You may, in fact, be surprised to learn how many ways you express tension, how ubiquitous it is in your life. Most of all, you see now that our first step, "Recognizing Tension," takes some careful work. Sometimes we're so used to being in a state of tension that we're unaware of its presence. If you'd asked Julia if she felt tense in the middle of her workday, she would probably not understand the question. More than likely she'd simply say she felt normal.

Triggers making us tense are so common we don't notice them after a while. But they have a cumulative effect. They automatically put us in an all-defenses-up stance. All of our agendas, our dogmatic beliefs, our deeply entrenched desire to guard ourselves from attack are instantly put into place when we feel tense. Tension prepares us to do one of two things: fight or flee.

Cultural differences can muddy the waters further. The "whirling dervish" emotional reactions that you saw in Mark are more common in certain cultures than they are in others. Mediterranean cultures (such as Italian, Spanish, Greek, Middle Eastern) seem to encourage the ready expression of emotion. Walk down the street of any Italian town and you'll probably hear a symphony of loud, free voices: angry, happy, crying. You have a great sense of emotional release: all feelings seem free to come out. Walk down the street of an English, German, or Danish town, and you're likely to notice the quiet. You have the equally strong sense that emotions have been reined in. This has more than a superficial effect, especially when you come from one culture and your partner comes from another. Our tension tactics of judging, blaming, wanting to "fix" the other person are almost inevitably triggered when one set of cultural expectations crashes into a different one. If you're American and travel in other parts of the world, you will often find that you're thought of as childish and naive, far too open in temperament, arrogant in your expectations that everyone ought to speak English, and ignorant in your reactions to what you see. When people from other parts of the world visit America, Americans often have different but equally judgmental reactions to cultural assumptions they don't understand or feel comfortable with.

All of this can roil the blood, make you tense, and make you retreat or lash out. The deeper our assumptions are, and cultural assumptions are some of the deepest, the more attacked we feel when they're not shared by someone else— and especially by an intimate love partner.

Step Two will give you a way to separate from this defensive stance so that you can begin to hear your partner in a new way. But Step One is crucial preparation. Just awakening to the fact that somewhere inside you an alarm has gone off can open the door to a whole new way of responding to that alarm.

What if you discover that you're in such a continual state of tension that it's still hard for you to notice it?

The best way to sensitize yourself to tension is to learn ways of experiencing the lack of it. Discovering what relaxation feels like, which you can do through meditation or any other exercise or activity that allows you a true feeling of calm, gives you something against which you can measure tension. (It will also prepare you for the second step, which, as you'll see, makes practical use of meditation.) The benefits of meditation are numerous, but in the context of doing the first step, its overriding benefit is that it teaches you, by contrast, what tension feels like. The more relaxed you can learn to be, the more aware you'll be when you're not relaxed. Like the princess and the pea, eventually you can sensitize yourself to the least discomfort: any flicker of tension will, after you've learned ways to *rid* yourself of tension, be instantly recognizable.

But perhaps the primary lesson of Step One is simply this: you learn that you can have a feeling *and not act on it.* Simply notice that you're having it. Allow yourself to tolerate, for the moment, its discomfort. The good news is that this discomfort won't last long, especially as you learn to employ the second step. The first step is really only a *moment* of recognition, a sign that it's time to move on to the second step. As you'll learn in the next chapter, the first two steps are almost simultaneous; their combined function is to allay anxiety, not increase it.

Let me reassure you about something else: the process of doing all seven steps isn't going to take all day or night. My clients and I have discovered that twenty minutes is about average for a complete intimate listening session, one that uses all seven steps. In fact, in most cases it shouldn't last longer: the intense focus of this process is best done in relatively small doses. As you'll soon see, a lot can happen in twenty minutes—or, for that matter, one, two, or five minutes.

In fact, five minutes of Step Two can give you more peace and understanding than you may ever have felt toward your partner. How? Let's find out now.

STEP TWO

CROSSING THE STREET

STEP TWO, "CROSSING THE STREET," means detaching your-self from the reflex to defend or attack so that you can give yourself time out to observe your partner's reactions. It's a crucial cooling-down step: you decide, for the moment, to put your anger, fear, and defensiveness on the shelf.

We "cross the street" in order to overcome any reflexive response to another person. A reflexive response simply means: every time he or she does X, you do Y (more than likely a repetition of exactly what you did in childhood). Only after we've checked our automatic responses can we stand apart and begin to hear our partners more objectively. Some-times we can do this only for a limited time. However, as you'll see from the examples in this chapter, even five min-utes of staying across the street can be a great help. If, after those five minutes, you've detached as much as you're able to, you can always return and yell, sulk, withdraw, rant, rave, or groan at your partner.

Which brings up an important point. There are always going to be times when you won't be able to resist losing your temper. Obviously our goal is to teach you to deal with your feelings in ultimately more productive ways, but few of us are saints, and sometimes we will lose control. Accepting these inevitable explosions—rather than berating yourself for not being able to control yourself—can, in fact, make it easier to keep your conditioned reactions on the shelf for a longer period when you next try the second step.

"Crossing the street" is crucial because it sets the stage for every step to come. Conceptually a simple step, it's not always easy to do. (For some people, it can be the hardest step of all.) It requires taking a brief meditative breath, and in the heat of anger or despair or any other charged emotion, meditation is often the last thing you feel capable of doing. But you can learn to adopt at least a momentary detached state more readily than you may realize. It takes practice, but it's worth the effort. Learning to detach from the steam of an argument is the only way to see what the argument is about.

Let's return to Julia and Mark to see the different ways they've approached this step of detachment. Later, we'll investigate other ways to cross the street. One or more of these approaches should appeal to you. As you'll learn, people with different temperaments cross the street in different ways. But the effect is the same: you become detached enough to hear what your partner is trying to say to you. After you've had experience being detached, you will probably find it pleasurable and empowering. A state of detachment means you're not taking on your partner's "stuff" so personally. Crossing the street gives you not only a sense of emotional neutrality, but also a sense of emotional freedom.

Certainly this was the case with Julia when she finally learned to do it. However, learning to cross the street presented some peculiar challenges for her.

Staying in the Room: Julia

When I said that crossing the street meant clearing the mind, Julia felt she was already a master at it; in fact, she felt she had been for years. "Clearing the mind" meant, to Julia, withdrawing—escaping into an inner world of safety where she could hide from the threatening world Out There—in this case, her angry husband, Mark. However, detaching doesn't mean you "leave" your partner. It allows you to be *more* present, not less. I didn't want Julia to escape Mark—I wanted her to separate just enough to feel less *enmeshed* so that she could tolerate being with him without bolting, lashing out, or withdrawing.

This idea of not "leaving" was, at first, very uncomfortable. Her usual pattern was to make a quick, scathing defense and then disappear. Now I was inviting her to stay in the room—mentally as well as physically.

She tried it at one of our couples sessions. Mark was on his usual rampage: "How do you expect me to trust you ever again? How do I know you're not having some new tryst right now? Okay, maybe I'm paranoid, but I can just imagine you telling Bonnie all about some secret affair when you see her privately, and now both of you are sitting there silently laughing at me." Mark glared at Julia. "You can't change the facts. You were a hypocritical cheat. Who's to say you're any different now?"

Julia's eyes flared—she said later that she could feel the tension rise in her chest. She "recognized" this tension (in other words, she did the first step) and then took a further leap. She decided to try to detach instead of lash out. She closed her eyes, took two deep, long breaths, and let her shoulders fall, relax. It took two, maybe three seconds. But when she opened her eyes again and looked at Mark, they didn't have their former angry, defensive glint. She seemed a little softer, a little more open. She had simply managed to become, as she described it to me later, "present."

These seconds of detaching from Mark's angry words were a triumph for Julia. She'd never been able to do this before. She told me later in her private session that it was almost a "high" to be able to *be* there so completely and yet not be afraid or angry. She'd allowed the meditation she'd been practicing on her own to affect her in the "real" world. She was discovering that she could make use of meditation right in the middle of Mark's attack.

This first instance of employing the second step followed Julia's attempt to meditate—or as she preferred to put it, "relax"—at home. At first, she told me, she felt silly. "I was around during all of that 'Me Decade' business," she said. "My friends did est. A roommate was into Gestalt and primal scream therapy. I remember one night at about three in the morning she scared the hell out of me when she suddenly yelled into her pillow and started punching her mattress. She said she was just getting rid of tension." Julia laughed. "Maybe it worked for her, I don't know. All I know is that she passed the tension on to *me.*" Another friend, she said, was into Buddhist chanting. Julia cringed at the memory. "I could never buy into any of that. I couldn't imagine saying *'om'* over and over again, lulling myself into some kind of serene stupor. All of that mantra stuff seemed like nonsense."

However, when Julia tried my suggestion simply to do breathing exercises—sitting up straight in a comfortable chair, inhaling and exhaling in a slow methodical rhythm— she felt calmer. "It was a little like going to sleep," she said, "except I was completely awake." Julia never realized how tense she was until she experienced this moment of relaxation. Her shoulders, neck, and back began to release a little of what she realized had been a perpetual "bunching up." "I couldn't believe what an effect this constant state of tension had on me, not just emotionally but physically. After a while, I could feel my whole body relax." Julia said she liked the word "relax" better than "meditate." "When you first talked to me about meditation, I recoiled. All I could think of were Eastern religions, which I don't believe in. But when I thought of it as relaxation, it didn't intimidate me."

Julia scheduled these periods of "relaxation" in the morning before Mark got up, when she could give herself ten, twenty minutes, sometimes as long as a half-hour alone. She learned simply to sit still and breathe slowly, allowing her mind to go blank. "Of course, it never goes exactly blank," Julia said. "I'm not some Zen master at this. But I don't obsess so much over what does go through my mind. I'm learning to just let it pass. And it really helps. I feel better after I've let it all go." She'd been on this schedule for a couple weeks before trying to do it in the room with Mark. At first, she said, "I was just too mad at him. I was sure I wouldn't be able to keep myself from blurting the same old defensive stuff back at him. But then I remembered something you told me."

What I had told Julia is that what Mark was expressing when he said he felt suspicious, angry, and hurt had to do with *him,* not her. His fault-finding and accusations all made it *seem* like it was about her. But it really wasn't. What he was doing was verbalizing his tension. Once Julia understood this, she could choose not to take the comments personally. She could—in the context of her "relaxation"—shift for a moment, and begin to hear Mark differently. "As much as I still resist the idea of a mantra," Julia said, "I started to chant to myself 'This is about Mark, not me' over and over. Combined with my slow rhythmic breathing, it sort of let me off the hook. I could truly *detach* from him for a moment. Not by white-knuckling it, or by repressing my desire to lash out at him, but by really letting go of that desire to hurt him back and then quickly shut down. I just didn't feel so threatened by him. In fact, for that moment, I didn't feel threatened at all. I could truly accept that what he was going on about had nothing to do with me. It had to do with his anxiety, his anger—with *him.* "

So, the three seconds Julia took to breathe were also three seconds of calming herself down with this reminder: "This is about my husband and his anger, not about me. Let him say it." What was the effect of all this on Mark? At first he wasn't aware of anything other than that Julia wasn't barking back at him and then shutting down in her usual manner. She was simply sitting there, looking at him. Then, baffled, he asked her, "What's wrong with you?"

Julia blinked. "Nothing," she said. And for that moment, it was true. Nothing *was* wrong. She'd experienced a moment of genuine calm in the midst of Mark's very noisy emotional storm. And she hadn't disappeared. For the moment at least, she was able to begin to hear and take in—without taking *on*—everything Mark said.

This moment is only the beginning of the rest of our process of "intimate listening," but it is a crucial one. And perhaps the most important point about this step is the last lesson Julia talked about learning: that what Mark was talking about had to do with him, with his state of mind. She had the choice not to take the bait, not to react to his accusations defensively. She could, for the moment, shift her stance and listen to him with detachment. She'd learned to cross the street.

This moment of detachment had another unanticipated reward, too. Julia felt emotionally freer than she had before. Her tension was, for this moment, truly gone. Whatever else she would learn to do in this position of relaxation, the stance itself was a comfortable way-station. Sometimes, in fact, you may not be able to get beyond Step Two—which may be just fine. Simply getting out of the tug-of-war, which Step Two enables you to do, can defuse not only your anger but also your partner's. When you're not taking the bait and lashing back at him, one of you isn't in the war anymore. Sometimes that's enough to get the war to stop. Not always, but sometimes.

There is of course more to do: we still have five steps to go. But the second step can give you a breather, no matter what comes next. That's one part of what Julia learned. Mark learned it, too—but after a different kind of struggle.

Dampening the Powder Keg: Mark

Mark, with his volatile, heart-on-his-sleeve emotions, faced a different set of problems from Julia in learning the second step. Remember what Mark said about himself in our discussion of the first step: "I always know how I feel and I've never been shy about telling anyone else. I don't understand these WASP types, like Julia, who hold it all in. I've never held anything in. When I'm angry, I blow up. When I'm sad, I cry. When I'm happy, I laugh." All this was a virtue to Mark: didn't his "open" emotions just mean that he was being honest? However, as we've already seen, his quick-trigger expression of every feeling he had was a kind of throwing up; emotions were something he felt he had to get rid of as quickly as he could. As he learned in the first step, this volatile expression was a kind of acting out that prevented him from *learning* anything from his emotions. Julia repressed; Mark expressed—but the effect was the same. They both escaped their feelings.

But now Mark understood that his urge to blow up was a sign of tension. This awareness gave him an instant of reflection, an instant to decide *if*, in fact, he wanted to blow up. Becoming conscious of this tiny moment of reflection was the beginning of the work he needed to do in the second step. He had to learn to extend this moment. He needed to learn that he could choose, again with practice (and the second step almost always takes practice), not to blow up *for now*—to shelve this urge so that something else could happen.

Mark hated the idea of holding himself in. He even felt there was something pathological about it: "Isn't that how people get ulcers? I don't want to deal with stuff like Julia does—push it down and have it eat away at me. What's the payoff for holding back my feelings?" Mark's reliance on blowing up as a technique for ridding himself of uncomfortable feelings was nearly total. It was part of how he allowed himself to feel safe. When I asked him to tell me more about the good of blowing up, he said: "It's like it'll *kill* me if I keep it in. My emotions are so strong they're toxic. Like some kind of terrible acid that will destroy me if I don't get rid of them."

Mark needed to realize that doing the second step—crossing the street—didn't mean he was permanently repressing his emotions. He had to understand that his emotional volatility was a trait and a technique that he had come to believe was the only one that could work for him. Accepting that it was only *one* of a number of possible techniques he could use would come with time. After practicing some form of Step-Two detachment or meditation, he could then start to try it out by degrees in the real world.

Self-compassion, however, was the first necessary step for him. Understanding and accepting that it would take time for him to feel safe without blowing up—that he wasn't a machine, that his escape hatch mechanisms were deeply rooted in his earliest childhood—allowed him to try, however tentatively, some new approaches. He needed to give himself permission to be patient: Step Two wasn't going to happen overnight for him.

Mark had learned to admit something important about himself from working on the first step: "I'm thin-skinned. It's like I lack some layer or buffer zone that everyone else seems to have between them and the world. I just don't seem to have that kind of protection against my feelings." Becoming conscious that this supersensitivity and tendency to overreact emotionally were part of his personality meant that he could work to control or change them.

However, moving from self-acceptance to feeling *calm* about being the way he was, was another question. The breathing exercises that had worked for Julia didn't work for Mark. He couldn't get beneath his feelings for long enough through this physical approach—he needed something that worked better on him *mentally*. In one of our private sessions, I had an idea. I asked him to visualize a circle of white light in the center of his mind, a circle that slowly, peacefully increased until it took up all of his head. He could allow this circle of light to dissolve any jagged, painful, or otherwise disturbingly colored thought, picture, or emotion with which it came into contact. The white light, I promised him, had a magical quality: it dissolved everything effortlessly, peacefully, with no resistance from anything it encountered.

Mark found this a comforting and effective meditation. Eventually he added to it the physical breathing exercise that Julia had used, so that the relaxation he sought could happen both in body and mind. But visualization was the most effective trigger for him. He needed a much more palpable picture to help him along than Julia had to gently dissolve his anxiety.

At first Mark wasn't as motivated to practice his meditation technique as Julia had been to practice hers. Partly this was because of a temperamental difference: Julia tended to "attack" new ventures conscientiously; her strong history of "best little girl" made her want to do things "right." Mark was more of an outward rebel: he didn't want to be coerced into doing anything that didn't promise immediate results or gratification. It was only after he associated the visualization with *pleasure* that he began to use it more often. "When I stopped thinking of it as some kind of New Age homework assignment," Mark said, "and began to see that it was actually making me feel good, I stopped resisting it so much."

However, because his feelings about Julia—his anger and hurt and defensiveness—were still so highly charged, he couldn't, for quite some time, imagine using this technique to detach from her. I suggested that he might want to try it out in other "real world" settings as practice for the second step he might employ later on with Julia. The idea appealed to him. One day he used his circle-of-light visualization before making a stressful phone call at work; later that afternoon he summoned it up again, dealing with an ornery paint salesman at a hardware store; at the end of the day he used it to calm himself in gridlock traffic. He was amazed: it worked. He felt calmer, better able to deal with things, not so angry or threatened.

Weeks after "trotting out my ball of white light during the day," as he put it, Mark attempted it with Julia in one of our couple sessions. Julia gave him reason to want to calm down. "I feel like I have to walk on eggshells with you," she said. "Every time I complain that you're not doing your share to help out with the house, you throw back the affair I had. It's like I can't bring up anything, even the mildest criticism, without you attacking me for being an immoral cheat."

Mark felt the usual urge to erupt, to lash back at Julia. Then he did his best to stop it. He allowed the white light to form in the center of his head. He allowed it to grow. He closed his eyes for a moment, urging it to grow larger. But certain words Julia had used—"not doing your share"—were lodged in the light like a black hole. He couldn't get beyond them. They made him furious. What did she mean, not doing his share? He worked as hard as she did. Just because he didn't get up as early on weekends as she did only meant he wasn't as obsessed and neurotic about the house as she was! As his fury began to increase, it burned away the fragile white light like the sun burns away fog. He opened his eyes; it was clear from the pain and anger in them that his visualization technique wasn't working. "How dare you . . . " he began.

Then he stopped again. He remembered something else he'd discussed with me about using the second step. It's a point I'd also brought up with Julia, although I haven't covered it here yet.

Switching Roles

By now, of course, both Julia and Mark knew what the second step was. It was no secret to Julia that, when Mark closed his eyes and stopped himself from blowing up, he was attempting to "cross the street." But, for the moment, he couldn't do it. The second time he stopped himself, it wasn't to try anymore to use the second step—he felt, right then, that detachment was beyond him. It was simply to tell Julia that he didn't feel he *could* "cross the street" right now. In fact, he said exactly that: "Look. I can't do it now, I can't detach from you. Please hear me about why."

This was a cue to Julia: he was inviting *her* to use the second step, to detach from him for a moment so that he could vent. But framing it in this way marked enormous progress for both of them. Mark was beckoning to Julia, in asking her to "hear" him, to cross the street herself, so that she *could* hear him talk about his own feelings. He was suggesting that real communication—distinct from the hurled insults they were used to in the past—*was possible* between them. Although he might even now frame his feelings as accusations, he knew from exploring the meaning of the second step with me privately that if Julia was able to cross the street, she wasn't going to take what he said personally. This was freeing not only to Julia, once she was able to detach, but to Mark: he could express himself freely with no worry about how it was coming across. If Julia was able to detach herself, she'd be hearing him differently—more completely, more objectively. He felt free to say whatever he wanted to say.

Of course, sometimes out of the hurt we feel, we *want* to hurt somebody else: Mark was certainly no stranger to this motive. But Julia didn't have to be hurt by his words even if he intended them to be wounding. She could—as later Mark could, when he felt more able to cross the street himself—

hear without taking what she heard personally. The important point here is simply this: Julia and Mark discovered that they could switch roles. When one of them wasn't capable of detaching from an argument, the other could try to do so instead.

But what if both of them weren't able to detach?

They could call time out. Julia could say, ''Let's shelve this until one of us is able to calm down enough to listen to the other, okay?'' In fact, Julia *was* able to cross the street in this particular instance. She could begin to hear more clearly what Mark's pain was all about. (You'll learn more about that pain, and Julia's too, as we go further into the steps.) And, in later sessions, when Mark felt capable of using his white-light technique, he discovered he could step out of his fury for a moment and listen to Julia's pain more clearly, too.

There are three general lessons to draw from Julia and Mark's experience:

1. You can decide to cross the street and listen to your partner without taking what he/she says personally.
2. If you can't calm down enough to detach, you can ask your partner to cross the street and listen to why you can't detach.
3. If neither of you can cross the street, you can call a temporary cease-fire—time out—until one of you *can* cross the street.

If this were all there were to our program, we'd be ahead. Steps One and Two defuse tension: they enable us to get out of the war and take a calmer look at what's going on. Of course, it's important to figure out what to do once you've called this truce. There are ways to reach each other we haven't begun to explore that the rest of our steps will make clear. However, if all you want to do is to cool down an argument, Steps One and Two—"Recognizing tension" and "Crossing the street"—are amazingly effective.

Different Strokes . . .

The technique you feel most comfortable using to enjoy the meditative breath of Step Two depends, obviously, on your temperament. Let's go over the personality categories we explored in the last chapter with a view to how each can adapt most easily to "crossing the street." One or more of them should work for you. In combination with what we've learned from Julia and Mark, the suggestions should enable you to map out a way to get across the street yourself more readily than you may think you can right now.

The Somatizer. You'll remember that somatizers translate their anxieties and feelings into physical symptoms. When you somatize, you may get a headache or diarrhea or become dizzy—or even experience seemingly purely physical ailments like arthritis—every time you feel tense, afraid, angry, depressed. Tension translates into physical pain: this defines the somatizer.

Someone I know who has had a nearly lifelong history of ulcers realized, as she thought about the second step and how she might use it with her lover, that it was her *expectation* that she would get physically sick when she was emotionally distressed that was almost the worst part of the experience. Anticipating pain is what crippled her the most. This is not an easy syndrome to get over. Like Mark and Julia, the somatizer knows how to deal with distress in only one way—the old way, by inducing physical sickness, discomfort, pain. But, on the evidence of somatizers I have known, there are some effective things you can do to block this somatizing reflex.

"What helped me," said a woman named Marian, "was a kind of pep talk I learned to give myself. I told myself I could push through the fear—and that I didn't *have* to get sick. I practiced telling myself when even the first stirrings of fear came up in me, 'You don't have to get sick. You're not doing anything bad. You're just having a feeling.' When I'm honest with myself, I know that the emotional trigger for me isn't just any vague distress; it's fear. Fear of my anger, fear of my lover's anger back at me—fear that he'll leave me, that I'll drive him away if I let out my feelings. Once I practiced letting out my feelings just a little bit, after a heavy dose of affirming that I didn't have to get sick, and discovered that the world didn't blow up and my lover didn't leave me, I began to have more faith that I could let out even more without getting horribly sick.''

Marian says that she feels she's on a sort of roller coaster—where she sees a big dip coming up, takes a big breath, allows herself to *whoosh* down, and then comes back up to a manageable plateau. When she sees her emotional life as this series of dips, rises, and plateaus it calms her: she sees that her life, her feelings, and her relationship with her lover *go on,* no matter how positive or negative her life may be at the moment. ''One thing I can count on, and something that's giving me more hope, is things always change. I'm not going to die if I let out a feeling. I don't have to get sick. It's only a feeling.''

When Marian faces a rough patch with her lover and gets to second-step territory, attempting to detach so that she can begin to hear him, she gives herself a moment to chant a reassuring refrain: ''Push through the fear; have faith; you're safe; it's only a feeling.'' This is wed to another refrain, similar to Julia's: ''This is about him, not about me.'' Like Mark, Marian has discovered that she benefits from trying this out not just with her lover when they're in a difficult conversation, but in less charged circumstances as well—dealing with testy salespeople, her demanding boss, her moody teenage daughter. The more she realizes that she *can* push through her fear and that she won't be destroyed by anyone else's negative feelings, the more confident she becomes—and the less her ulcer acts up.

If you tend to somatize, try thinking of your emotional life as an ongoing stream with ups and downs, a stream that may bring you every possible emotion but won't destroy you. Remind yourself that you will survive, you're safe—you can ride this stream wherever it takes you. And take a cue from Julia: remember that what you're hearing from your partner has much to do with him or her, not necessarily with you.

The Overly Cheery. We've already seen in our discussion of excessively cheerful people in the last chapter that one of their main motives is to take away somebody else's pain. Like the somatizer, the excessively cheerful person can't tolerate anyone else's negative emotion. When the eternal optimist says things like "It's all for the best" or "Tomorrow's another day" he is often desperately applying first aid—mostly Band-Aids, but anything to stop the black emotions hurtling toward him. In fact, you understand this type of personality best when you realize that all of the cheerful person's energy is directed to dodging what seem like poison bullets—the anger, distress, discomfort, sorrow, depression of anyone else.

Andy, a man of middle years, was this kind of determinedly cheery person. He betrayed the anxiety he was feeling beneath all of his sunny optimism by eating compulsively: he would go through a box of chocolate-chip cookies, a pint of Häagen-Dasz ice cream, and half a cheesecake nearly every night. He wouldn't allow the world to see his anxiety, and it had to go somewhere: in his case, it went into eating. But to hear him talk, he hadn't a worry in the world. He was so happy he had the positive approach to life he did. He couldn't understand depressed people. Why didn't they just snap out of it, look on the bright side? Andy's cup was definitely half full, not half empty. Norman Vincent Peale was his patron saint.

Taking a positive approach to life is wonderful. But Andy

needed to see the fear, anxiety, and fierce self-protective urge that his "positive" exterior was hiding from him. Unconsciously, as suggested by his nonstop eating, he was in an almost continual state of distress. A change occurred when I asked him to describe how he thought he'd feel if, one evening, he didn't resort to his usual after-dinner desserts. What if he skipped a night, fasted? Or what if he just had a small apple and a glass of water? How would that make him feel?

At first Andy laughed—he couldn't imagine it. He'd never not indulged his sweet tooth. But then a change came over his face: he looked perplexed, then worried. "It would be horrible," he said slowly, softly. "I couldn't bear it." In this darker emotional moment, I asked him how he felt when his wife nagged at him, something he said she did every day, especially to get him to lose weight. Always, before this, he'd passed it off with a comment like "Oh, that's just the way she is. I still love her. She doesn't really mean anything by it."

But now he gave me a different and truer picture of his feelings. In fact, it was Andy who gave me the image of "poison bullets." "It's like she's shooting at me," Andy said in the same slow, soft, sad way. "Some poisonous gun where, if the bullets touched me, I'd die. My only protection is my optimism—it's like a golden shield the poison bullets can't get by. That's why I'm always so positive. I mean, if I make my wife think I'm fine, and keep telling her not to worry, things must *be* fine, mustn't they?"

Andy realized in this moment how much his cheery facade *was* a facade. I suggested a meditative exercise that would help him to do the second step the next time his wife started to nag at him. He could continue to imagine being "protected" by the bullets he felt coming from his wife, but he didn't have to put up a shield. Instead, he could start thinking of them as completely harmless. The bullets were made of air. He could simply allow the bullets to go by. He had no need to defend himself. They had no power to hurt him.

Andy tried this visualization; eventually it took. It became for Andy a kind of meditative reminder, one that allowed him to "stay present" (to use Julia's phrase) without resorting to a barrage of "happy talk." He could just simply *be* there when his wife got angry. Visualizing her "bullets" as illusory, as little bits of air, worked for him: it drained the venom out of her nagging, allowed him to hear her in a different way.

If, like Andy, you have a tendency to look on the bright side that verges on desperation, you're not going to want to hear that the world isn't as rosy as you want it to be. Even if you do make the connection that something about your non-stop optimism is defensive, you're probably not going to want to change that defense: it works too well. But think: does it? What negative feelings are you pushing down? What behavior might these repressed feelings be causing you to adopt? Maybe, like Andy, it's overeating. But it could be anything: oversleeping, overworking, substance abuse, excessive attention to detail, procrastination.

If the overly cheery description fits you, try following Andy's lead. First of all, allow yourself to talk about what *does* distress you. Maybe just talk to yourself at first, or with a friend or therapist (you'll probably want to save your partner for later when you feel stronger), but give it a little play. Realize that if you talk about your negative feelings, not everyone will automatically think worse of you. It's human to feel these feelings. Practice accepting these darker, more fearful parts of yourself. With time, your fear of them will lessen. Then, like Andy, when you perceive yourself under attack, feel free to imagine yourself as completely protected: what's being thrown at you are words, *air,* with no power to hurt. Give yourself time to practice this feeling of being "defended" without becoming defensive, not only with your distressed or angry partner, but also in other difficult areas of daily life. Soon you'll see that you don't have to expend so much effort spreading sunshine. The sun will still be there, even if a few clouds, a storm, or a period of darkness obscures it for a while. Doing the second step for you, no less than for our somatizer Marian, means having faith that the sun will come out again—without your having to *do* anything about it. Inducing this feeling of calm may come from visualizing "poison bullets" and detoxifying them, turning them into harmless air. It may come from one of the more purely physical modes of meditation, like Julia's deep breathing exercises. See what works for you, and then try it out, in small doses, until you're able to "cross the street" with your partner.

The Perfectionist. Perfectionists almost invariably have a lot invested in getting "the facts" right. This obsession with accuracy can give them a hard time with the second step. One recovering alcoholic client of mine, Beth, tells me frequently how angry her husband makes her because he always gets the facts wrong. "I know exactly what we did last Sunday, what the weather was, what I was wearing, what he was wearing, what his mother said—you name it. But when he tells a story about last Sunday, he gets everything wrong. I *know* it was sunny; he says it was raining. I *know* we left the house at five—he says we left it at seven. It's like that famous song from *Gigi* with Maurice Chevalier and Hermione Gingold—'I remember it well.' Well, the hell *he* does. He doesn't remember a damned thing. I wish it didn't bother me so much, but it drives me nuts."

For Beth to accomplish the second step, she had to tell herself, for the length of "intimate listening" time she would spend with her husband (and I reminded her that it was never to exceed twenty minutes): *Facts don't exist.* "I imagine we're in some sort of Alice's Wonderland," Beth says. "I tell myself I don't have to correct him. *It doesn't matter* how much nonsense he invents. And it's funny—when I finally, deeply give myself permission to have it *not* matter so much, I can't tell you the relief I feel!"

As much as Beth resists the idea of crossing the street and

letting her husband say whatever he wants (however inaccurate his facts may be), when she finally is able to do it, she often discovers she likes it there. "I guess this is the revelation," Beth says. "All the energy I expend trying to get things right, making sure things go exactly according to the way I've planned them, is *exhausting*. So when I can allow myself, meditatively, to cross the street, I usually find I like it better. It feels good to give up control for a while." Beth sighs deeply, as if to punctuate this revelation; you can feel her relax even as she imagines the relaxation she experiences when she does the second step.

Of course, Beth is happy to hear from me that she's allowed to get back to her "facts" after her twenty-minute session of listening intimately to her husband. "I do love the feeling of letting go that the second step gives me," she says, smiling. "But I still like getting the facts right." She looks to me for reassurance. "I guess I can have it both ways, huh?"

The Blamer. People who blame other people or situations as a reflexive way to get rid of their anxiety often feel the same relief that Beth felt when they're able, via the second step, to give up their attachment to blaming. Often, blaming someone or something else is a way of denying a secret: down deep, *you* feel guilty—and more deeply, powerless. It's very common for faultfinders to discover, as they look at their own childhoods, that they always felt impotent in the face of critical parents—that "it was my fault." Blaming is often a way of getting rid of this hidden guilt by projecting it onto someone else. Unconsciously, the blamer is keeping her own guilt feelings at bay, getting rid of them as fast as they come up by throwing them outside onto others.

Jack, a client of mine who through therapy has come to realize that his urge to blame is a defense against his own secret feelings of guilt ("I was a classic, brought-up-by-strict-nuns Roman Catholic," he says. "I feel like I caused the Vietnam War") came to feel wonderful relief when he learned to do the second step with his girlfriend. "My girlfriend is always late, and I'm always blaming her for why I'm anxious—we never get anywhere on time because of her!" I suggested that he attempt to "cross the street" the next time he felt the urge to argue with his girlfriend, by repeating to himself the mantra "For the next five minutes, nobody is to blame for anything." When he really registered this, when he really allowed it to go deep into his mind, he experienced the same pleasurable letting-up that Beth experienced when she allowed her husband to get the facts wrong, to be as inaccurate as he wanted to be. "For the first time, I felt free," Jack reported. "While I was supposedly giving my girlfriend a break, I was giving myself a break. It was like being in a whole new world. Certainly I heard her differently. But I also felt different myself. I felt more powerful."

To some degree, we're striking the same note we've struck in our last few categories: whatever message it means giving yourself, or whatever meditative method it takes, it's a *relief* to cross the street. It not only enables you to hear your partner differently, but also frees you emotionally. Discovering that we can exist without entrenched defenses is liberating. It's a psychological axiom that we move toward pleasure and away from pain. That's why the second step works so well: after a while, you *want* to do it (even if it *is* good for you).

The Advice-Giver. There's one aspect of defensive dynamics we haven't explored yet, one that's particularly true of people who can't keep themselves from giving unsolicited advice. Advice-givers often feel they have to be everyone else's parents. In fact, you can radically change your perception of "advice" simply by realizing that the advice-giver is almost always talking to himself—often parroting what his own parents told *him* to do. This can revolutionize how you listen to your partner (or your mother!). Just imagine that every bit of advice ostensibly aimed at you is really directed at the advice-giver. You'll never hear him or her in the same way again.

But what if *you* are the chronic advice-giver? As with every other category we've explored, you generally experience great relief when you give yourself permission—as you do in the second step—to cross the street, stop being the parent, and simply listen. Like the overly cheerful person, advice-givers think they have to fix things. But even more than the cheery personality, the advice-giver thinks it's his or her *responsibility* to fix things. In fact, the advice-giver's secret belief (and worry) is that the world can't go on *without* his or her advice.

This is an exhausting way to live. The advice-giver shares the obsessive/compulsive's desire for control, but adds to it a hefty dose of *me*-ness: a weary, parental "If I don't do it, nobody else will." For the second step to work, the advice-giver has to agree to give him- or herself a vacation from this sense of responsibility. And, as we've seen with other personalities who've managed to give themselves permission to cross the street, doing this can be a huge relief. One advice-giver I know repeats to herself before she reacts to her "inept" husband: "I'm taking a vacation, I'm taking a vacation, I'm taking a vacation. . . ." She visualizes a beach in Aruba, settles herself into the warm sand, listens to the soothing waves; she can now regard her husband placidly. She doesn't only cross the street—she puts herself on the beach! But again, whatever it takes, the point is for the advice-giver to give him- or herself permission to cease giving advice. That's the only way the second step can happen.

The Moralist. Again, we're in familiar territory. People who are judgmental, who can't walk down the street without morally condemning the hemlines and makeup of women passersby, the mercantilism of Christmas, the unthinkable sloppiness of their neighbors' unraked lawns, not to mention the thoughtlessness of their spouses . . . well, you get the picture. It's no picnic judging everything all the time, and the judger needs to find a way to take a vacation from judging if he or she is going to manage the second step. But it isn't easy.

In some ways moralists have it the worst of all; they face the most difficult obstacles in allowing themselves to cross the street. Judging means defending a moral code. How could you turn your back on your morals, even for an instant? Such an idea is unthinkable to the moralistic judge.

Let's not feel too smug: most of us hold some fierce moral beliefs we can't imagine questioning, much less changing. We all find it difficult at times even temporarily to leave our morals behind in order to hear our spouses more clearly. Witness Mark's ongoing pain and feelings of betrayal in the wake of his wife Julia's past affair. He can't give it up, and he doesn't want to. In fact, he feels it would be *wrong* to pardon Julia's behavior even for a minute! You don't have to be a religious fundamentalist to know what the "judger" feels. Just go back to any terrible feeling of betrayal or injustice and you've located an area of your own fierce judgmentalism.

But it is still an obstacle. Moralists need especially to accept that the Second Step is part of an experiment that serves the greater good: communicating with your partner. In fact, one of my more judgmental clients uses this very idea in a second-step meditative phrase: "It's better for the moment *not* to judge than it is to judge." You might also do a variation on the familiar "Let he who is without sin cast the first stone." We all know what it is like not to live up to some standard, to fall beneath our own or somebody else's expectations. Moralists need to induce in themselves at least a temporary stance of forgiveness. Doing the second step may also mean becoming a bit more humble. "Cross the street" because you want to increase your understanding of something you don't yet understand perfectly—your partner's behavior.

It is clear by now that these personality categories overlap. In fact, it's probable that you see yourself in more than one of these descriptions—maybe, at different times, in every one of them. But the basic message of the second step is: let up on yourself. Relinquish control. Reserve judgment until later. Get out of the war and walk to a neutral side: cross the street. As you've seen, this is accomplished by various forms of what can be called meditation. I can't give a primer on meditation that will work for everyone. Some people (like Julia) are turned off by the very word; "relaxation" makes more sense to them. Some people discover that visualization works to calm them down, as when Mark visualized the circle of white light or my advice-giver client put herself on a beach in Aruba. Others find that physical breathing exercises or even regular sessions with a good masseur can induce the right kind of relaxation, a relaxation you can learn to take with you when you face your partner. Experiment with different meditative approaches—then use what works for you.

You've also learned that employing this second-step period of relaxation or meditation we call "crossing the street" takes practice. Remember that you're bucking lifelong defenses; you're changing some of your most entrenched behaviors, defensive patterns you've relied on all your life to "save" you. And sometimes, as we saw with Mark and Julia, you just can't do it. What you *can* sometimes do when you've hit a block is switch positions: invite your partner to cross the street and listen to you. If neither of you can do it, call time out. Table it until later.

The more you use the second step, however, the safer you begin to feel—as safe as you used to feel hiding behind your defenses. By practicing the art of being calm, you're doing more than putting yourself in a better position to hear and understand your partner. You're giving yourself a break. So join my advice-giver client in her imaginary Aruba. There's plenty of room on the beach.

SUGGESTED BOOKS ON MEDITATION TO HELP YOU "CROSS THE STREET"

The More We Find in Each Other: Meditations for Couples, Merle Fossum and Mavis Fossum (Harper San Francisco/Hazelden, 1992)

The Art of Being, Erich Fromm (Continuum, 1992)

Reflections in the Light: Daily Thoughts and Meditations, Shakti Gawain (New World Library, 1988)

On Having No Head, D. H. Harding (Viking Penguin, 1988)

Buddha's Little Instruction Book, Jack Kornfield (Bantam, 1994)

A Gradual Awakening, Stephen Levine (Anchor/Doubleday, 1989)

Meditations from the Road, M. Scott Peck (Touchstone, 1993)

STEP THREE

ENGAGING THE OUTER EAR

STEP THREE, "ENGAGING THE OUTER EAR," means following your partner's line of thinking, absorbing his or her words verbatim. You listen carefully, without judging. When you feel the urge to defend or attack, you stop yourself and simply repeat back your partner's words in the form of a question, so that he is invited to explain what he means by them. What you're doing is allowing the whole flow of what your partner wants to say to come out. You also discover that you can survive what your partner is saying (you learn that it won't destroy you).

As I mentioned earlier, I base this approach on social psychologist George Kelly's work in the 1950s; he argued that the specific choice of words reveals one's own "personal construct": our strings of sentences hold the key to how we perceive reality. Later steps will help you to unravel these strings so that you understand more of what your partner is really saying. Once you realize that more is going on beneath your partner's words than either of you realized, and that what you may have once perceived as a personal attack may have little to do with you (based, as it usually is, on childhood patterns of distress that long predate your relationship), your tension and defensiveness decrease. You'll be able to defeat your "fight or flight" reflexes. The result? You become a more objective—and less threatening—listener; your partner feels safer and thus becomes more open and revealing as he talks to you.

But Step Three is just the beginning of this process. Once you've shelved your volatile feelings at least for a limited period (which you've done in Step Two), you are able to hear your partner in a new way. Emotions are replaced by uncharged attention: you absorb your partner's words like a sponge. You listen to silences as well as to words (as poised and observant as a fisherman waiting for a tug on his line), without offering any interpretation or opinions of your own.

Step Three illustrates an important truth about initiating productive communication with your partner: the responsibility for creating a safe communications "space" isn't up to the speaker, it's up to the listener. Once you've created that space through becoming an intimate listener, you have set the stage for a miracle: your partner will begin to speak in ways you've never heard before. You'll both discover truths that were long buried or disguised. Getting this far is a gift.

Julia and Mark's experience will point out a number of important techniques and challenges involved in engaging the outer ear; later in this chapter we'll again explore a variety of personality types to see how each can best deal with some particular "outer ear" Achilles' heels.

Julia: Letting Him Fill the Circle

By the time Julia and Mark got to the point of employing the third step with each other, they had to deal with a new and disturbing circumstance. For business reasons, Julia had to plan a return trip to Chicago—the scene of the "crime," the city both Julia and Mark associated with her extramarital affair. It took both of them all the persistence and meditative techniques they'd learned about in the first two steps to talk to each other about this development. Suddenly they were plunged again into the worst of the threatening feelings that had rocked them so badly before.

However, because they'd practiced the first and second steps assiduously by this point, they were able, with effort, to go further into the third step—"engaging the outer ear." Happily, the experience of this step turned out to be more healing than either first believed it could be.

During one session, Julia and Mark began by carping at each other that neither was "available" enough: job pressures had kept both of them working overtime, and Mark especially felt that they'd become merely roommates, passing each other like the proverbial two ships in the night. What made the tension especially great, however, was the prospect of Julia's Chicago trip.

Julia knew this, but she also wanted to try the third step as a means of dealing with their—and now, specifically, Mark's—tension about it. She was able, meditatively, to cross the street before questioning Mark about his own feelings. She told me later, when I saw her alone, that she'd followed my advice to create, in her imagination, an immense circle fully occupied by Mark—for the moment, she was going to cease to exist, except as the barest peripheral presence, a tiny sliver of light on the edge of the circle. She allowed Mark, his words, his feelings, his presence, to take up the entire space of her mind. It was his turn now to speak—and, she told herself, it didn't matter what he said. With the clarity and distance she had achieved via the meditative second step, she was able for the moment to blank out her own apprehensions.

Following another of my suggestions, she kept her questioning to the fewest words possible. Again, she wanted to intrude as little as she could on the "circle" Mark now fully occupied. The whole point was to let Mark's own light shine through.

This wasn't easy. As Julia told me later, she decided to open her mouth to speak to Mark only after undergoing a considerable silent editing process. At first she wanted to say to him, "I notice you're putting up roadblocks. . . ." Then she changed it in her mind to "Tell me why you're putting up roadblocks. . . ." But this, too, she realized, was too belligerent and would invite nothing but Mark's defensiveness. Then, she said, she remembered something she'd told me about how she perceived Mark: "It's like he's a burn victim. You have to handle him with the gentlest, least intrusive care for him not to lash out." Thinking of him as this pained burn victim, she now saw her words as the barest, softest touches of a puff of cotton.

Mark repeated his last question: "How could you think of going back to Chicago—don't you know how this hurts me?"

"Hurts you?" Julia repeated softly.

"Well, of course! It's where it all happened," Mark said. "I'm really scared that you'll have an affair again. You'll lose your inhibitions."

"Inhibitions?" Julia gently parroted back.

Mark was still on a rampage, but the hardness in his eyes abated a bit—he looked a little surprised that Julia wasn't jumping down his throat. "Look—you're going back to that city, to the hotel you met that guy in, you're seeing him again in a business meeting. How could you not be tempted?"

"Tempted?" Julia said.

"Well, yeah. Hell, *I'd* be tempted. . . ."

"You'd be tempted?"

Mark paused a moment, frowning thoughtfully. "Whenever there's distance between us," he explained slowly, haltingly, "it's not only your leaving me that I worry about. I feel so shut out that I . . ." He paused, sighed, then continued: "Oh, what the hell. I feel like turning to someone else too! I can't stand being shut out. And now that you're not only going away, but going to that damned city—the very word 'Chicago' makes my stomach tense—well, I'm worried that *I'll* be tempted to cheat on *you.*"

Julia had struck gold. By allowing Mark to let 'er rip a bit about his feelings, it emerged that he was worried about his *own* impulsiveness, the pain of his own loneliness driving *him* to seek comfort from someone else.

Of course, the third step is meant to elicit words only from the speaker; it is the art of amassing data. This wasn't the time for Julia's reactions to be expressed; later on (in the fourth step), she would allow herself to reflect on what she was hearing in the conversation and begin to unravel her reactions to herself. But there was no denying that important data had emerged: they now shared an insight that much of Mark's anxiety and distress about her extramarital affair had to do with his own impulses to stray. Later, when Julia pondered more about her husband's neediness, she thought to herself, "If Mark doesn't feel completely embraced, all the time, encircled by loving arms, he feels totally abandoned. For him, it's one extreme or the other. He can't abide any separation."

These observations, she would learn, could be tested as she went further along in the process of the steps. But now it was her turn to occupy the circle, and Mark's turn to listen.

Mark: It Doesn't Have to Hurt to Hear

Julia's perception of Mark as a burn victim is telling: we've already seen how his first impulse in the face of any strong feeling was to leap away from it. It was as if feelings were like flames: getting too near them even for an instant was unbearable.

We've also seen how this reflex made it particularly challenging for Mark to do the first and second steps. How can you learn to stay with feelings you find so threatening? Mark had made strides: because he was now able, with practice, for longer and longer periods, to stay "across the street," he was also learning by degrees that he could tolerate emotions more than he once thought he could. He had discovered how to create useful protective boundaries. He was also helped by responding to Julia's questions when she employed the third step with him: he'd managed to speak about difficult feelings that he'd barely, before now, articulated to himself. And she hadn't jumped down his throat. He began to entertain a new idea: maybe you *could* say what you felt and have it be safe.

In this calmer state, he turned the tables and attempted, as his wife had done with him, to listen to her without intruding.

He asked her, "How do you feel about going to Chicago?"

"I don't know," was Julia's impatient response.

Mark paused, fighting a strong impulse to go on the attack. "How could you not know?" he wanted to shout back at her. He told me later that he experienced Julia as willfully withholding when she came up with equivocal responses like this one. It maddened him. But he held himself back, marshaled his "calm" back into place, and parroted her as unobtrusively as she had questioned him: "You don't know?"

"I always feel like I have to come up with some kind of correct response with you!" Julia shot back. She was still angry, and visibly steeled herself for an equally angry reply from Mark. But, for once, Mark wasn't taking the bait.

"Correct response with me?" he asked.

"Dammit, you *know* you put pressure on me to say what you want to hear. If you don't hear endless reassurance, you fly off the handle. Don't you understand? *I'm not lying:* I really *don't* know what I feel about Chicago. Beyond feeling bewildered and . . . scared, I guess. I don't want to mess things up, but . . . well, what I'm really dreading, if you want to know the truth, is talking to you on the phone while I'm there, talking to you when I come back. I can't stand your suspiciousness. It just shuts me down. I never know what to say to you. I never know how to persuade you that I'm not the conniver you seem to think I am. I really *don't* know what I feel a lot of the time, except pressure, from you, from the office, from everybody in my life. I want to shut down. I want *out.*

That's probably why I had that affair. It was something that I thought could take me away from all this pressure. . . .''

Julia's outburst was highly unusual. She had revealed more in one flow of words than she ever had before—at least to Mark. The sheer quantity and force of her feelings, of her words, astonished him but, he was amazed to realize, did not make him feel defensive. He genuinely wanted to keep her talking. And so, on cue and without affect, he was able to repeat to her her last word: "Pressure?"

"You don't know what it's like. It's been this way my whole life. It's like I never have the chance to figure out what I feel because there seem to be so many guns at my head, so many expectations to fulfill, so many people to placate and make happy. You want to know what I feel about going back to Chicago? Scared. Scared of my own suggestibility. You know I'll have to see that guy again at a business meeting. I feel terribly uncomfortable about it. But maybe I'm most scared . . ." Julia paused, furrowed her brow as if grappling with a new thought. "Maybe I'm most scared of your anger. Of your mistrust. Of your hating me."

"Hating you?"

"Well, isn't that all you've communicated to me? That you hate me? No wonder I shut down. If you feel hated, you don't exactly want to open up. I don't have a clue *what* I'm feeling half the time, except guarded and shut down. You don't know that I really do love you. You don't know how afraid and confused I am about that affair, how guilty I feel. You complain about feeling disconnected, but I don't think you have any idea how disconnected I feel. Not just from you. From everybody. I'm like this lone asteroid out in space. That's as close as I can get to telling you how I feel. Totally alone."

Julia began to cry softly. Mark was overwhelmed. He had never heard her say these words before.

Presenting Julia and Mark's experiences with the third step is in one sense artificial. As you'll see in the next chapter, they each segued without a beat into the fourth step—"Activating the inner ear," attempting to listen imaginatively, freely, with the aim of making connections that would clarify the meaning of the words they'd amassed from each other. But, for now, let's stay with this first opening-up—examining the data-gathering of the third step so that we can understand as clearly as possible what it entails.

What amazed Julia and Mark had to do with the wealth of data that seemed to be bursting to come out of each of them. Merely by questioning each other without anger, without expressing any interpretation of the answers, they had each unlocked some enormously potent and important feelings and information. What enabled this data to emerge? As Julia said to me later, alone, it was simply this: "I didn't take the bait." What she meant was, she allowed Mark to say whatever he wanted to say without allowing it to push her usual defensive buttons. And Mark was able to do this with Julia, too. They now had intimate data that would profoundly change their understanding of each other. And it all happened by getting out of each other's way, letting each other produce an uninterrupted flow of words, feelings, self.

Different Ways to Engage the Outer Ear

Let's take a look now at the challenges each of the personality types we've identified before faces in employing the third step. As usual, you should find a number of "shoes" to fit you, and a number of techniques that should resonate with your own circumstances and experience.

The Somatizer. Somatizers, who translate their anxieties into physical symptoms, often benefit from relying sheerly on rote technique, learning to trust and keep as closely as possible to the mechanics of the third step. These, as we've seen, are simple. Parrot back the last couple of words your partner has uttered in as neutral a tone as possible.

One allergy-stricken somatizing client of mine, a woman who was trying to employ the first three steps with her husband, said she felt particularly blocked. She experienced her husband as Mark experienced Julia—aloof, withholding, shut down. However, when she was honest about her feelings of being shut out, she had to admit she was actually afraid of breaking through his barriers. "I now see that I'm terrified of the boundaries between us dissolving. As much as I complain that I can't get through to my husband, I guess I have to accept that I've made sure there *is* distance between us. I mean, I'm in conflict over it, or I wouldn't be bringing up in therapy our lack of communication. But I'm afraid that if he really lets me know how he feels, it will destroy me. It's not just that I'm afraid of his turning against me—I'm even afraid to hear that he loves me!''

Like Julia, this woman feared any expectations at all—she felt inadequate to the task of living up to any other person's view of her. And so she took out her feelings on her own body—keeping them within the boundaries of her own self, asking nothing from anyone else, including her husband, except sympathy. "Sympathy is all I seem to want, or am able to accept, from anybody," she said.

This woman had particularly powerful and painful experience with overstepping boundaries: as a little girl, she had been sexually abused by her stepfather and was working through her rage and terror over this in private therapy. However, she was able to employ the third step as she became more comfortable with the idea that all her husband was going to give her was "words," which (unlike sticks and stones or sexual abuse) didn't have to hurt her. She also experienced comfort with the step by learning that she could rely entirely on its mechanics. She could help to elicit data from her husband by extremely simple means: parroting back a few of his own words. She didn't have to extend herself in any other way. She sought and found refuge in the simplicity of this task. And the bonus was, her husband began to talk to her and to open up to her in a context that threatened neither of them.

If you tend to somatize, you may find similar comfort in sticking to the rote mechanics of the third step. If you're the speaker and your partner is questioning you, you can also find safety in the boundaries of this technique: your partner can't harm you with his words; neither can you harm him with yours. Like both Julia and Mark, it will help you to learn that you *can* tolerate direct expression of emotion; you don't have to become physically distressed by it. In fact, more than tolerate it, you can learn from it.

The Overly Cheery. The overly cheery person often hides a secret, indeed unconscious, terror: if he or she really starts to listen to the partner, the partner will disintegrate. This may sound far-fetched, but consider the experience of a client of mine. He's a relentlessly upbeat, jovial, overweight man who, through private therapy, was able to express some of the apprehensions he had about his wife "getting mad at me." "I can't stand the thought of her being angry with me," he said. "And I've just begun to realize, now that I've talked about this fear with you, where it comes from. My mother would go into rages when I was a little boy. I didn't know then that she was dealing with a bipolar disorder—what used to be called manic depression. Without warning, she would get very high or very low. All I knew was, she would suddenly, and for no reason, explode at something I'd do. It made me terrified of her anger. She seemed to fall apart—almost literally. She'd tear at her apron, mess her hair up with her hands, throw pots and pans. I felt it was my job to cheer her up. No wonder I'm so cheery today. And I guess I'm afraid that my wife will blow a fuse and fall apart if I ever let her express all of her feelings."

My client needed to learn that he could tolerate the unexpected, and that (again) all he was eliciting from his wife in the third step was *words*. He began to realize that his fear of her going out of control was unfounded as he allowed himself, first for very short periods of time, to listen to his wife in the controlled, third-step way. Sometimes all he could manage was a minute or two of this kind of listening. But the more he tried it, the less threatening the process became, just as the more you practice the meditative techniques of the second step, the more they'll work for you.

If you tend to be overly cheery as a defense, you may find that practicing the third-step listening technique in the same progressive way (starting out with short periods of listening, lengthening them as you feel more comfortable) will similarly calm your fears. You'll learn that it's not your job to keep your partner from going out of control or disintegrating. If you're the speaker and your partner is questioning you with the third step technique, be similarly patient with yourself. You and your partner are both much more resilient than your old fears want you to believe.

The Perfectionist. As we've already seen in previous discussions of this personality category, the perfectionist usually feels compelled to get the facts right. It can be particularly hard for him or her to cross the street and permit his or her partner to speak freely—the impulse to correct is a hard one to fight down.

One client of mine, a recovering alcoholic who's been sober for ten years but still has ''control freak'' tendencies, says that the reason she is such a perfectionist, and such a hard taskmaster with her lover, is that she feels so shaky inside. ''After a lot of years of self-examination,'' she says, ''I know that my obsession with getting details right comes from a deep feeling of chaos—it's like, if I don't maintain absolute vigilant control over everything and everyone in my environment, the whole universe will come toppling down.'' She knows that part of this comes from being herself the child of alcoholics, having had to deal with the inconsistencies and wild mood swings of her parents: ''They made me feel like I was supposed to be a certain way to get their approval—but I never had a clue what 'way' that was, because their demands kept changing unpredictably, they were so contradictory. I didn't know that this was typical of drunks. As a little girl, all I knew was that I kept getting it wrong.''

The good news is that Step Three can actually change the perfectionist's life! As this woman put it, ''Once I realized that the main rule to follow in Step Three is *not* to comment on anything—that debate wasn't allowed—it actually freed me. I felt the first relief I think I've ever felt listening to my partner.'' As we saw with the second step, giving yourself permission to ease up on your expectations may at first be unnerving but finally can be a great relief. It's the same thing with the third step. ''I don't have to *do* anything,'' my client says, ''besides gently prod my partner to speak freely. Letting him off the hook means letting me off the hook.''

Look to the third step as a way of freeing yourself from the burden of your own perfectionism and expectations. The rewards of this can be incalculable, not only because they include giving your partner freedom to speak, but also because they give you freedom from having to exercise control.

The Blamer, as we've seen, has great difficulty tolerating his or her own guilty feelings. Blamers' reflexes may be to blame others, in fact to guilt-monger and make others wallow in their unbelievable stupidity, but what they are usually battling internally is the feeling that *they're* the guilty party. Scratch the surface of almost any blamer, and you find a very guilty ''inner child.'' This is borne out by many of my clients who have come to realize that they tend to blame as a defensive reflex. One young man who knows he complains about everything—the pushy people on the subway, the slow cashier at the supermarket, his unbelievably obtuse boss, not to mention his self-absorbed and uncaring wife—as a defense against entrenched early childhood beliefs that *he* was worthless. ''The more I talk with you about how awful I felt as a kid, the way my father would berate me for everything I did, my mother fuss over every mess I made, I realize I grew up feeling guilty for everything. And the idea that I'm projecting all this guilt outward, blaming everybody else, makes more and more sense to me.''

What this young man has realized as he practices the second and third steps, is that his impulse is to regard any information from his wife as a scaldingly hot potato: ''If she says anything negative about me, it calls up how awful I felt as a kid when my parents chewed me out, and I feel like I've got to lash back.'' But as he repeats the second step mantra we talked about—''This is about her, not about me''—he finds himself more able to do the third step. ''I'm learning that I don't have to react to anything my wife says as a hot potato. I'm learning, in fact, that it's neither hot nor a potato! It's nothing at all—nothing, at any rate, that I have to react violently to. The data my wife gives me when I use the third-step listening technique is simply that: data. I don't have to do anything about it beyond simply recording it.'' Or, if he's the speaker in the third step, simply saying it.

The Advice-Giver. Like people who blame or are overly cheerful, advice-givers generally react to information from anyone else as a threat—something to ''fix,'' get rid of, surmount. Advice-givers rarely indulge in long, relaxed verbal exchanges. How could they? When you react to every bit of information you hear as a desperate cry for help—help you're convinced only you can give—there's not much chance you're going to be relaxed about it. Advice-givers typically are exhausted.

As we've seen in the second step, when advice-givers finally learn to give themselves permission not to be everybody's parent, they generally find tremendous relief. To one self-confessed advice-giver client of mine, I've suggested emphasizing the pleasure aspect of letting up on this feeling of parental responsibility: ''Practice not giving advice!'' I've advised her. "Enjoy the pleasure of letting everyone fall down and bump their knees and find their own ways." Letting go of this sense of responsibility takes practice, but the rewards of doing so are as relieving to the advice-giver as they are to the blamer. They also serve the greater aim here, which is to allow your partner to speak.

When the tables are turned and advice-givers speak in response to their partners' third-step questions, they can expect, at first, to feel tongue-tied—as if they have nothing to say. Secretly (like the blamer), they regard their own thoughts— which they almost never reflect upon for any length of time— as a signal to others to "fix" them. Learning, slowly, that words can simply be words—that nothing need be *done* about them, they can simply be said—is usually as great a relief to the advice-giver as learning that he or she doesn't have to advise anyone else.

The Moralist. In some ways, moralists have the hardest time doing the third step. Why? Because their opinions are heavy with morality: people who judge other people generally feel they would be immoral not to do so.

What I suggested about the second step is equally true of the third: moralists need especially to accept that this whole process is part of an experiment that serves the greater good— communicating with your partner. But something else is important, too. If you know that you tend to be a moralist, you may benefit from entertaining the idea that *you* deserve as much compassionate attention as you're attempting to give your partner. (This will especially help you if you're the speaker responding to third-step questions.)

One client of mine says she was always known as a "Goody Two-shoes." "Kids in school didn't like me," she said. "They thought I was stuck up, when really I was just being who my parents told me I had to be. I wasn't allowed to chew gum, to get my clothes dirty in the playground, any of that. I was always apart from other kids. And later on, in high school and college, when people were drinking and having sex and doing drugs—well, forget it. It just wasn't in me to break the rules like that. I grew up a strict Catholic. The only way I knew how to navigate the world was to play by the rules I'd learned—rules that I'd been told God wanted me to follow!''

But sticking to the straight and narrow sometimes made her feel heartbreaking loneliness. ''I was never invited to parties. I went out on very few dates. I had, really, very few friends.'' Why was she so strict with herself when it cost her this dearly? Lately, she has begun to understand that she was protecting nothing less than her identity: ''It was who I thought I had to be—who I still think I have to be. I learned there's a right way and a wrong way to do everything. I didn't think I could be in the same room with a person who said or did 'sinful' things—it would somehow contaminate me!'' This has been the problem she's faced in attempting to listen to her husband, who in her view lapsed incomprehensibly and unforgivably. ''I found out from his lawyer, who called the house once when my husband was out, that my husband had been married before he met me. Because of my view of divorce—I don't believe you *can* be divorced, not in the eyes of God—he didn't dare tell me.'' It has been very difficult for this woman to transcend her gut aversion to discussing the topic, to even begin the process of neutral listening in the third step.

''It's only been recently that I've been able to give myself permission to let him talk,'' she said, ''and that's come about after a lot of prayer and self-examination. Part of it, I realize, is that I love him more than anyone in the world, and that love gives me some kind of power to forgive him. But I'm also starting to forgive myself. I've kept myself in such a cage my whole life, I'm not sure what I truly think and what I believe because I've been told I'm supposed to believe it. I haven't come close to sorting that out, but I've been humbled by trying, and the very least I can do is listen to my husband. The neutral territory of the third step appeals to me. It gives me the first space I've ever known where I can meet my husband without judging him.''

Like the perfectionist, this woman and many other people who share her reflex to judge also find comfort in the very strictness of the third-step listening technique (whether as listener or speaker): it requires that you *not* judge, that you take in without taking *on* the words your partner says to you. As with every other personality we've investigated, you generally feel profound relief shelving your anxiety for the time it takes to do the third step. And, after submitting to the entire process of the steps, you may find when you look back up at that shelf, that your anxiety has disappeared—or at least assumed manageable proportions.

I said when we investigated Julia and Mark's experience of the third step that there was something artificial about separating it from the fourth step—''Activating the Inner Ear''—which follows it. As essential as it is to gather the raw data of your partner's words, obviously the aim is to understand as fully as possible the realm of *meaning* that data reflects, which the fourth step will begin to help you to do.

However, just as you never entirely leave the second step behind as you go through the rest of the steps—you may continually need to remind yourself to ''cross the street'' when something your partner says starts to irritate you—you never leave the third step behind either. Whenever your feeling of neutrality is threatened—when something your partner says stabs into you even as you're trying to hear it merely as ''words''—you can step across the street and position yourself to begin listening with your ''outer ear'' again. In other words, these steps are *renewable*. When your partner's words threaten to start the usual chain of emotions and bickering, you learn that you can stop, pause for breath, and, simply by listening, reroute the discussion in a more positive direction. Listening with the outer ear is the only way you'll be able to go further—to begin to understand who your partner is, and what he or she is trying to tell you.

STEP FOUR

ACTIVATING THE INNER EAR

STEP FOUR, "ACTIVATING THE INNER EAR," means listening with intuition to sift through your partner's words so that you find the key thoughts and phrases that will convey his or her meaning to you. It is not only listening without judging, but also listening with imagination—allowing your mind to wander freely, to free-associate, to absorb on a deeper level what your partner is saying. You try to see the connections your partner is making as he or she speaks, attempting to open up to what may lie beneath the surface of the words.

Sometimes the first three steps of our communication process are all that's needed to resolve a conflict with your partner. But you may want and need to go deeper. Some basic misunderstandings persist even after you've made the attempt to listen with detachment—by crossing the street and engaging the outer ear. You may need to sift further for clues, to discover hidden meanings, to resolve tensions from the past to make a more loving connection to the present. This is the process that "Activating the Inner Ear" initiates.

Now that the intuitive listener has gathered the data from the first "outer ear" stage of listening, he or she learns to view other people's speech less as sentences than as collections of words and phrases that are keys to the shadowy halls of the speaker's mind—keys to secrets that may be locked even from the speaker. All the speaker may initially be able to say is "Something's bothering me." The intuitive listener can begin to uncover what that "something" may be.

Most listeners have little experience truly *hearing* anyone. The more usual impulse is to try to reason the speaker out of his or her statements. This makes the speaker defensive and a war often ensues, one partner defending, the other attacking. Trying to answer the speaker "logically" can also turn out to be an ineffective tactic. "Logic" often stops us cold and sends us back to our shells. We keep our deeper and more tentative thoughts and feelings—what I call "tender, private information"—closely guarded. We feel that these thoughts are too fragile, often too connected to feelings of shame, to withstand the onslaught of persuasion or argument.

What we secretly long for is someone with the patience and care to listen without arguing. The fourth step enables you to become that rare and longed-for listener. Advice has no place in this stage of intuitive listening, of activating the "inner ear." In this chapter, I'll offer techniques to help you encourage your partner to free-associate, to let his or her imagination go free, to encourage a gentle and more nurturing atmosphere.

As before, we'll first see how Julia and Mark managed to use this step for some good examples of what you are likely to face in your own attempt at intuitive listening. Then we'll explore our personality profiles for additional "inner ear" challenges and techniques.

Hearing the Dream: Julia

When Julia heard Mark say that *he* was afraid he'd stray when she left on her business trip to Chicago, his admission frightened her. Suddenly the tables had turned: now she was anxious, jealous, and afraid in anticipation of Mark cheating on her. For her to employ the fourth step, helping Mark to reach for past connections, she had to distance herself once again from the threatening feelings Mark's admission had engendered in her. I suggested that she use a specific technique to do this—one that has proved remarkably effective with many other people when they attempt the fourth step.

When Mark said, "I have an urge to stray," I suggested to Julia that she hear this as if Mark had said, "I had a dream that I had the urge to stray." This little mental sleight of hand is effective because it diminishes the threat—making it seem less likely that Mark will act on his impulse—and it's really more accurate. Mark's urge is still in his head, his imagination; it is very much as if he *is* recounting a dream. Julia could listen to Mark more openly, letting in his free associations in the same way that she might listen to him talk about his dreams. This would help her keep from taking what he said so personally, and would guide her to help Mark express even more associations, just as a therapist might do in encouraging a patient to free-associate about the imagery of a dream.

This brings up another important point: *Step Four happens in the* **mind** *of the listener.* The work of this step is silent. Julia had to train herself to free-associate, to listen with imagination to whatever Mark said. No longer was she simply amassing data, as she had done in the third step. Now she would allow her mind free rein—to infer from what Mark said the deeper meaning of his words.

Julia's external technique was the same as it had been in the third step—simply repeating Mark's last word or two in a question to keep him talking. But what she was doing *inside* was much more active. She said to me later that she kept asking herself: "What am I hearing?" This, she said, kept her on track. Here's how the process worked, both inside and outside:

When Mark repeated that he was afraid of his own "urge to stray," Julia echoed him: "Urge to stray?"

"I just don't want to play the fool," Mark said. "With you back in Chicago, getting tempted again—maybe giving in again, it just makes me look like a chump. I feel like I have to get back at you.''

"Back at me?'' Julia repeated. By now, as she later told me, she'd visualized Mark as a cranky, abandoned baby in a crib, howling in frustration and sadness and fear. The words "stray" and "chump" somehow became linked to her: she saw the baby Mark again, crawling down a path, crying, lost, with other cruel kids looking on from the sidelines, jeering at him. She began to *feel* what she imagined Mark was feeling, not just to hear his words.

Mark paused and seemed to shift gears. "Yeah, I want to get back at you. But . . . it's more than that. I just realized something uncomfortable. I think I also want you to feel sorry for me.''

"Sorry for you?'' In Julia's mind, the baby Mark suddenly sat up and looked around him for sympathy.

"Yeah,'' Mark said quietly. "It's like what I do a lot at work. I'll let everyone else maneuver for the best office, say it doesn't bother me that I'm not getting one of the larger corner offices with windows. You know that old joke 'Don't mind me, I'll just sit here in the dark.' '' Mark looked down at the floor. "Boy, this is hard to admit. But I think I want everyone else to commiserate with me. I want them to comfort me.''

In Julia's mind, the baby Mark was now in a cold, dark room, hugging himself. "Comfort you?''

"Yeah,'' Mark continued, subdued. "Fat chance of that happening. You know, at least you have some friends you talk to. I don't really have anyone else. You always seem like you're getting the better deal.''

"The better deal?'' Julia saw the baby Mark haul himself up to his feet, clenching his hands into fists, challenging the world.

"Yeah,'' Mark said, "you and everybody else. Maybe I'm even a little paranoid about it. I feel sometimes like everyone else is getting what they want, and joking about me not getting anything, because I'm too—I don't know—*stupid,* maybe, to figure out how to get anything.''

Julia had a complex little baby in her imagination by this point: she heard Mark say that he was not only afraid of appearing the fool, wanted people to feel sorry for him and to comfort him, but also resented those same people for always getting "the better deal." She had begun on a gut level to *feel* these contradictory emotions and thus to understand Mark more empathically than she had before. In fact, as Mark later discovered with even more force when he employed this step with Julia, Julia felt the urge to comfort him right now—to break out of her listening stance, to reach out to hold him and reassure him. But she realized that Mark still had more to reveal. Comforting Mark right now would have stopped the flow. As difficult as it was for her to hold back, she knew she must do so in order for Mark to go forward. All she needed to keep her empathic understanding of him as a feeling was to be silent for the moment—to keep it in the realm of the imagination, of a "dream," so that she could help Mark get even closer to the source of what was really bothering him.

We've already seen that holding back or keeping himself contained is not something Mark was ever comfortable doing. His experience listening to Julia in the fourth step was tumultuous for him, but immensely illuminating—not only about Julia, but about his own capacity for intimacy.

Scuba Diving vs. Snorkeling: Mark

Mark began to employ the fourth step by using the same "as if" technique Julia had used: he heard Julia's last statement, "I feel like a lone asteroid out in space," as if she had said, "I had a dream that I was a lone asteroid out in space." He was helped in this by Julia's vivid dreamlike imagery: he could, he later told me, actually *see* that asteroid, a tiny twinkling dwarfed by infinite, cold, black space. He felt how cold it was—and was able to feel how cold and alone Julia must be feeling, too.

The imagery and the feelings elicited by it were in fact so strong that Mark gave in to his own urge to cut them off. He couldn't hold himself back: "To hell with this fourth step business," he blurted out to Julia. "I feel so terrible for you. I never realized how alone you felt!" Jolted back from her dreamlike state, Julia seemed, at first, grateful for Mark's sympathetic outburst. Her eyes softened and she smiled at Mark. But she was silent. It was as if someone had abruptly and violently shaken her awake, and she'd lost her bearings. Although she saw Mark's expression of empathy as "loving," she also felt profoundly disoriented. Deep down, she knew she wanted to cover more territory. Mark's outburst kept her from doing this.

As difficult as it was for him, Mark seemed to decide to be quiet again. As he later told me, he realized that he'd cut things off prematurely: Julia wasn't talking anymore—he'd cut off the flow. He made the conscious decision to attempt, once again, to tolerate his own discomfort at Julia's discomfort so that she might continue talking, free-associating. So he took a deep breath, crossed the street again, set himself up to listen with his outer ear, and softly repeated Julia's last words:

"Out in space?"

Julia was silent for another long moment. Mark checked his urge to prod her with more words. It was as if she needed to find her own way back into the trance she'd been pulled out of. "Out in space," she repeated herself, this time with a soft, bitter chuckle. "Yeah, that's me. You want to find ol' Julia, just look in the blackest corner of the universe. Good heavens," Julia said, drawing herself up, "I certainly sound pathetic, don't I?" She closed her eyes, then opened them. "If only I knew what the *rules* were . . ."

Mark suddenly flashed in his mind onto the picture of a schoolroom: Julia stood in front of a classroom, red and flustered because she couldn't remember the words of a poem she was supposed to recite. "Rules?" he asked.

"Yeah," Julia said, now in a tone of disgust. "Why can't things be simple? Why can't I live like my parents brought me up to live? Why don't I want to have a child?"

Mark was brought up short: this last question seemed, in fact, like the "lone asteroid" Julia had described before, only now it was crashing through the roof, totally unexpected. He and Julia had talked vaguely about starting a family sometime, when the house was fixed up and their financial situation was more stable, but it had always been stuck in the foggy, general "future." In his mind, the classroom transformed into a nursery with an empty crib. He couldn't see Julia in this room; he could only hear her voice. He repeated: "A child?"

"Isn't that what we're supposed to have? I mean, why get married if you're not going to have a family? You might just as well have one affair after another. I don't know . . . I'm so confused. . . . I don't have a clue if I even want to have a child. I just feel so burdened . . . like we're supposed to be starting a family because that's what the rules are. But what are the rules? What is it we're supposed to be doing? What am I supposed to be doing?"

The nursery had turned in Mark's imagination into a cyclone, the crib and Julia and Julia's parents and the broken boards and furniture of their house and Mark himself all caught up in it, like in *The Wizard of Oz*, swirling around in chaos. "Supposed to be doing?" Mark managed to repeat.

Julia didn't say anything for another long moment. Then, after a long sigh, she said, barely audibly, "If only I could make some *contact* . . ." Another pause. "Maybe when I go to Chicago we can, I don't know, set up a schedule where we talk to each other on the phone in the morning and at night, just to make *contact*. I can't get any more specific about what I want than that. I just want to feel like there's somebody out there who can *hear* me. Please, please, just *hear* me. *Be* there. Be at the end of the phone when I call. Don't judge me. Just be there. Listen. . . .''

The cyclone calmed down, the debris settled. Mark saw Julia standing in the midst of the debris, calling out to him, looking for him. It occurred to him that he'd never before allowed himself to go through the full before-during-and-after process of a "cyclone." In his mind, freely visualizing what Julia's words brought up in him, he'd allowed himself, it felt for the first time, to go through the full arc of a feeling. He hadn't bolted in his usual panicky way. He'd stayed with Julia throughout. And in his mind, his "dream" of Julia standing in rags in the middle of the debris left by the cyclone, he could imagine walking through the ruins toward her. It was an unnerving experience as he recalled it. He hated cyclones. And yet he had survived one.

As I've stressed in our exploration of all the steps so far, it is the listener's task to become invisible, to allow the speaker to command the stage, to take up all the space. However, sometimes, and often during the fourth step, you'll have a revelation about your *own* response, as Mark had here. Mark knew that as much as he craved intimacy, he was also terrified of it. "I feel like I've only ever snorkeled," he told me in a private session. "Stayed up at the surface looking down, afraid—in fact, because of the snorkel, *unable* to go any deeper. But when I allowed myself to free-associate in the fourth step with Julia, I realized I'd traded in the snorkel for scuba-diving gear. Now, with my 'tank' full of imagination, I could go places I'd never gone before. I could stay with her even as she drew me deeper and deeper into her own heart and mind. I still wasn't comfortable doing this, but in some ways, it was wonderful. I felt closer to her than I ever had before.''

Again, it was Mark's task in this step to keep Julia center stage, and indeed, as he progressed through the next three steps, he was able to do just that. But as he reflected later on his own response to employing the fourth step with Julia, he'd learned something important about his own capacity to go "deep," to experience, tolerate, and even cultivate deeper intimacy. The listener stays backstage, but he's not untouched. The process the listener allows to take place in the speaker is one that transforms both of them.

For the moment, we'll leave Julia and Mark in the rich, intimate territory they've allowed each other to enter, except to note one interesting detail: in her free associations, Julia stumbled onto a very concrete and workable suggestion for lessening tension between her and her husband during her trip to Chicago. She suggested that they make a schedule of phone dates to keep up contact. Later on, she and Mark could decide to implement this suggestion. However, right now, the listening process had to continue. It was still too early to plan any kind of action.

Personality Types and Their "Inner Ears"

Let's now explore what other personality types face when they attempt to listen with their "inner ears."

The Somatizer. The first thing the somatizer needs to do before attempting the fourth step is to congratulate him- or herself for getting this far. It has been no easy task to rechannel energy so that it doesn't manifest in the same old "diseased" ways. The somatizer somatizes—expresses feelings through bodily complaints—out of deep, entrenched habit. If you've managed to turn this habit around, even a little, you've made enormous progress.

What the somatizer needs to cultivate continually is an empathic connection to him- or herself. Whenever you feel tension, or blocked from "crossing the street," or unable to listen with either the outer or the inner ear, stop for a moment and acknowledge this tension—in effect, repeat the *first* step as often as you need to. To truly empathize with your partner, to allow yourself to free-associate without feeling threatened, you need, continually, to remind yourself that you'll be *safe* doing this. One of my somatizing clients, an allergy-ridden woman who knows that her illnesses are stress-related, says she manages to listen to her husband with her "inner ear" by imagining that what he is saying is a movie that she has the power to cast as completely as she wants. In other words, when her husband talks about his frustrations with paying child support to his first wife, she immediately envisions a big movie screen where her husband appears as an actor acting out a script that has nothing to do with her. This is a variation on the "think-of-it-as-a-dream" technique we've seen Julia and Mark employ. But it has the advantage for this somatizer of keeping her husband's feelings distant enough to tolerate, yet vivid and affecting enough to allow her to hear and "see" them imaginatively. So, if you somatize, try using this movie technique. Make yourself casting director, camera operator, and audience—but allow yourself to be as fully inspired as possible by the "script" your partner is giving you. You'll find yourself employing your imagination and increasing your empathy in ways that don't threaten you or bring on one more bad headache.

The Overly Cheery. As we've seen before with this personality, his or her greatest fear is of the *dark* emotions. One overly cheery client of mine told me how terrified he was of his wife's admission that when she gets depressed and she's home alone with the kids, she sometimes feels like "reaching for the kitchen knife and . . ." Of course, she never finishes the sentence, because Mr. Joviality has cut her off with some palliative like "Oh, honey, you know you don't really feel that way. Let me tell you this joke Harry told me. . . ."

Just as the somatizer needs to go back to Step One, recognizing tension, the overly cheery person generally profits from resuscitating Step Two, "Crossing the Street," repeating a mantra like "This is not about me. This will not destroy me. I can tolerate this." Dark feelings, like "light" feelings, are normal, instructive, and far more tolerable than the overly cheery person expects them to be. Think of feelings as a kind of mental weather, indicating that there may be a disturbance, but guaranteed to pass. In fact, this overly cheery client of mine, once he's returned as often as he can to the other side of the street, finds himself visualizing his wife's words climatically: when she gets dark, he sees the clouds roll in and the rain pour, when she gets calmer, he sees the late afternoon sun deepening into dusk. This climatic visualization keeps him close to his wife's feelings, but translates them into something he can tolerate imagining. He can thereby free himself to hear his wife without cutting things off with a laugh and a joke.

The Perfectionist. After experiencing the profound relief of the third step, in which the perfectionist has finally managed to extract himself from his own perfectionism—and that, as we've seen, is indeed a great relief—the fourth step can sometimes invite the old compulsion to "get things right" back in. The perfectionist needs to step up the inner message he's given himself in the third step, that there *still* are no right and wrong answers, that in interpreting his partner's words intuitively, he can still stay out of the picture, allowing the partner's feelings to lead him to his visualizations. One recovering addict client of mine says that it helps him to think of his partner's words as a horizontal line, a tale that goes on and on with no special climaxes, peaks and valleys, or lessons to be learned, but rather one episode leading into another into another. He says his normal impulse is to think "vertically," searching above or below for the "right way" to rate whatever he's hearing or experiencing. But imagining the flow of his partner's words as linear and ongoing frees him, he says, from this vertical urge, and keeps him from butting in with his old "You've got the facts wrong" critiques. Doing this also increases the sense of liberation he's begun to feel in the second and third steps. "It's amazing," he says, shaking his head, "how relieved I am to stop doing what all my life I thought I loved to do: catch other people getting their facts wrong. It's like I've always thought competition was how you had to do everything, from pushing to be first on line at the supermarket to getting the biggest bonus or raise at work. It's not that there isn't some kind of thrill doing that, but it's also incredibly exhausting. I can hear my lover now when I let up on that jagged, up-and-down grasping for 'the prize,' and simply let it flow like a river. That's how I visualize her words now: a stream I don't have to do anything to but look at and dream about."

The Blamer. Once the blamer really registers that every word out of his partner's mouth is not a scalding hot potato, he too almost always experiences enormous relief. One chronic faultfinder I know, a woman who in private therapy is working through some terrible pain as the result of her having been sexually abused as a child by an uncle, says that, with her husband, she can listen intuitively only when she imagines them sitting across from each other at a kitchen table. She imagines a warm, sunny room where they've both just had a wonderful breakfast; but the table is the most important part. "I need to feel that there's some distance between us, I guess. Not a cold distance, but one that allows us to sit up, alert, receptive, but *safe*—no touching allowed. I know this comes from what I'm dealing with from my childhood, needing to feel I've got safe boundaries between me and whomever I'm with, but the combination of the sunny, comfortable feeling of the kitchen and the distance of the table allows me to relax and let my mind flow. I'm safe in this warm environment, and I can let my imagination go with whatever my husband says to me. I suppose this is like the meditative technique of imagining the most comforting and beautiful place you can, somewhere you're able to go in your mind whenever you need to feel peaceful. That's what my imaginary kitchen does for me. It helps me to accomplish Steps Two, Three, *and* Four."

What the blamer needs to cultivate is the feeling that whatever is said is just *fine*. The feeling of guilt that every blamer is trying to run from in him- or herself is like acid: it can eat through serenity in an instant. You may find, like my client, that imagining a perfect safe place will help you to let go of guilt and blaming; in fact, the more you return to it imaginatively with your partner the more you will associate talking with your partner with *safety*. The point in the fourth step is to release the imagination, which is admittedly risky business. Sometimes dark and threatening feelings are evoked by your partner's words; you may be led to visualize some frightening things (remember Mark's gut feeling of despair when he "saw" Julia's lone asteroid in space, and how difficult it was for him to tolerate the picture). You need to feel you're on some kind of island of safety before you can let your intuitive powers free. But when, as my client with her ideal of a warm kitchen demonstrates, you find this island, you can feel like you're home free. You have the delicious experience of everything being *okay,* even as you're gaining new and deeper insights into your partner.

The Advice-Giver. The advice-giver often experiences the same urge to express empathy that Mark experienced with Julia when he cut off the process of the fourth step: "I never knew you felt so alone!" In fact, it is tremendously difficult for the advice-giver to hold back from expressing opinions about what he or she hears: it's hard to pass up an opportunity to "fix" things. The advice-giver is appalled by the very idea: how could it ever be permissible to hold back all this helpful love? Less consciously, the advice-giver may feel threatened by the emotions the speaker has revealed; the advice-giver sometimes cannot bear to get any closer. Giving advice is as distancing a tactic as it may appear, sometimes, to be a loving one.

What the advice-giver needs to realize is that sometimes holding back a response, however loving and empathic the advice-giver may perceive it, can ultimately *increase* his or her capacity for love, and the capacity to express it to the speaker. Something important we haven't stressed thus far about the effect of Step Four on the speaker is simply this: the speaker learns that she can say whatever she wants to say. By demonstrating that you're not going to jump down your partner's throat, even with the best-intentioned advice or sympathetic "I know's," you're allowing your partner to see that you can tolerate whatever they come up with. You are demonstrating that your love is not bound by conditions: you're still *there* no matter what your partner says. You're not being destroyed by it. Your partner is not being destroyed by it. You can survive this expression of feeling.

It is a general truth, which the advice-giver reflexively ignores, that most people don't want advice when they speak. Like Julia, most people simply want to be heard, want to *feel* heard. When the advice-giver truly makes this connection, truly registers that every word his or her partner speaks isn't a crying-out for advice but is rather simply a *release,* the advice-giver (like our other personalities) can feel a release, too. But the most important message advice-givers need to give themselves is that holding back can sometimes be the most loving reaction possible. And, in terms of the fourth step, holding back enables you to get out of your partner's way and words. Remember: your task is to free-associate, listen intuitively, make connections based on what your partner is telling you. It may at first feel like you're not doing enough. But you are. You're in the process of forging a much stronger and more productive connection to your partner—by quelling the urge to butt in.

The Moralist. As you now know, and especially if you identify yourself as a member of this personality category, staying out of your partner's way and words in the manner we've been encouraging throughout this listening process can be tremendously hard.

What you need to return to is something we identified in the last chapter about Step Three, listening with your outer ear. You need to have faith that there's more to be learned than you know already. Even if you're sure you're "on the side of the angels," you need to take a leap into the unknown—just for the moment—and attempt to feel what it is your partner is feeling without judgment.

The religious woman I spoke of in the last chapter, who discovered by accident that her husband had divorced a first wife, had, like so many of the other people I've described, to bring herself back to Step Two, "Crossing the Street," to re-infuse a meditative state. She said that what helped her was the sense that putting her moral beliefs on the shelf served a greater good: she was giving her husband the opportunity to learn more about his own feelings, something she could not have done if she had simply dismissed him out of hand as "immoral." "In a way, what I learned," this woman said, "is that it was immoral to place myself on higher moral ground at least for the duration of using these steps with my husband. The rule was that he was allowed to have his say— and that it was my task to help him, by the least intrusive means possible, to say it. And when I began to listen to him intuitively in the fourth step, my heart couldn't help but soften. I saw that he had gone to such lengths to hide his divorce from me because he loved me so much. He knew how devastating it would be for me to accept him as a divorced man, and he couldn't bear the thought of losing me over it. As I visualized and emphatically felt his fear, as I put together the motives he expressed in hiding from me, I saw him with more compassion and openness than I ever would have been able to do if I'd stuck to my old straight-and-narrow 'Don't even talk about it, there's no discussion possible' stance. Don't get me wrong—divorce is still not admissable in my moral scheme of things. But it's not so easy now to ignore the emotional impact that my husband brings to the picture. It tears my heart apart sometimes to think how afraid and alone he's felt keeping this to himself. And I've learned all this by sticking to the 'rules' of the steps: nudging him as gently as possible to free-associate, and then free-associating myself with his words, staying out of it as I listen to him. I don't know where we're going to come out in all this, and it's hard to keep the faith that we'll be able to get through it intact. But I guess I can't help having a wider view of possibilities than I had before. One thing I know: I love him. And I'm willing to keep listening.''

As you've seen in every person we've talked about in this book, so much of what these steps invite us to do is to shelve our habitual responses so that we can allow our partners' thoughts and responses full expression. This means turning around some often very entrenched habits. However, as I hope you've also seen, the rewards can be extraordinary. You almost always find, as you listen to your partner, a whole new person—a fragile, tender, feeling self hidden under the surface. Step Four teaches us to listen to this hidden self without barging in, so that we can go even deeper. Now that you've begun to make associations, and begun to make acquaintance with who your partner really is and what his or her feelings really are, you can add more pieces to a bigger jigsaw puzzle.

In Step Five, the picture gets even larger: these ''hidden selves,'' that you're discovering in your partner and that your partner is discovering in you, have a lot more to reveal.

STEP FIVE

REACHING FOR THE PAST

STEP FIVE, "REACHING FOR THE PAST," means encouraging your partner to link his present circumstances and feelings to feelings and events he experienced earlier in his life. With the clarity and data the first four steps have given you, you're ready to delve deeper, to allow your partner to make connections he may never have thought to make before, connections that usually turn out to be surprisingly revelatory. The questioner's task in Step Five is to ask a simple question: "When did you feel like this before?" Eventually your partner should be able to make some illuminating connections. For example: "I always felt this way when my mother nagged at me" or "My father always made me feel I wasn't good enough—just like you're making me feel now." This connection-making does something crucial: it shows you that much of your partner's reaction has nothing to do with you. You discover the old battles he's fighting in the guise of complaining about or attacking you. Both of you begin to see the larger picture, to better understand the sources of what's bothering him.

What you often find when you encourage your partner to make these associations is that his fears, resentments, confusions, and doubts are connected to his earliest childhood memories. Step Five enables you to help the speaker bring more of these old patterns up to consciousness, which in turn will help him sort out what is a negative reflex connected to feelings of powerlessness that he had as a child and what might be more appropriate choices of feeling and behavior that he has the power to make as an adult, today. All of this is in service of allowing your partner to open a door to the past that he or she may have slammed shut. Traveling through that doorway can reveal important information about the source of the blocks that hold your partner back today.

Each of us has unresolved tensions from the first relationships we knew (mainly with our parents, but also with siblings, relatives, and other significant people we knew in earliest childhood). We all survive childhood by choosing certain adaptive paths, but these adaptations often cover underlying wounds that are left unhealed. In adulthood, as we connect in intimate love relationships, these wounds open up. If we are received welcomingly, nondefensively, we have the chance to heal past damage with our lovers. We do this by projecting an early conflict onto the present relationship. In the context of adulthood, we can use our developed sensitivities to sort out what the problem may be in the present and what may be an old family "film" replayed out of context. We begin to see whether in fact we're mad at our lovers or merely have unfinished business with our mothers or fathers.

This is the kind of work you begin to do in Step Five—the work of remembering and sorting out past from present. Let's start, as before, by investigating how Julia and Mark were able to open their own long-shut doors to the past, and then explore other personality categories for more clues about how to nudge these crucial associations and connections out into the light. As you'll see from all of these examples, and from your own experience when you try this step, that the illumination "reaching for the past" provides can be astounding.

Helping Mark Reach for the Past: Why Do I Feel Stupid?

In employing the fifth step, Julia concentrated on a recurring word and theme Mark had given her throughout his responses so far: the fact that he felt "stupid." This revelation amazed her. "As much as he's admitted sometimes that he felt he got a raw deal—his parents weren't good enough, he never felt like he was accepted by anyone else, from schoolmates to his first two wives, he was always quick to say how smart he was," she later told me. "How he was the only one in his classes in school who never needed extra help, who always had his hand up first, who was always able to one-up his competition. I'd never known before that he secretly saw himself as 'out of it,' 'stupid.' "

So Julia took this as a cue. She asked Mark: "Were there any times in the past when you felt stupid?"

Mark responded with a snort. "No! I was always the smartest kid on the block. What I'm going through now has nothing to do with the past. This is completely new." Mark's tone and demeanor had changed utterly; he was angry at Julia. "What're you trying to do, play shrink?"

Mark's defenses had roared up, and their reemergence tells us something important. You will often meet with resistance when you first start the fifth step with your partner. This is touchy territory. Mark's anger at feeling "psychoanalyzed" might have occurred anywhere along the third and fourth steps, and it offers us an important red flag. The questioning in the third, fourth, and fifth steps has to be done in a spirit of genuine interest, feeling, intimacy. You are not cross-examining a defendant. You are gently beckoning to your partner to explore his feelings and share them with you. As much as you need to be detached, you also need to convey the message that you're not cold or completely uninvolved.

It's certainly true that the techniques involved in these steps are good psychological strategy; in fact, I use them with every patient I see. But I'll tell you a secret: sometimes they *don't* always work in my private life. Sometimes I see that I need to back off, change my tone, or examine my own motives in questioning to see if *I'm* being defensive and communicating that to my partner. When, for example, I attempt to use these steps with my husband, and he says something like, "Save it for your patients!" I know I need to reevaluate the situation. It's not that I'm necessarily doing anything wrong. It may just be that my husband isn't ready to go deeper than he already has. As we said at the outset, sometimes all you can accomplish are the first and second steps—simply allowing yourself to get calm and cross the street. The point is: be sensitive to your partner. Don't barrel in with "technique" when you can see that your partner is not receptive to it. There'll be time in the future to try again.

However, Julia managed to change gears and salvage things by saying this: "I'm sorry, Mark. I don't mean to be coming across as a shrink. I'm just really interested in this. I've always seen you as smart. You've always described yourself as smart! But you've just admitted that you feel stupid sometimes. I care about you—and I want to know more about why you feel like this." She paused. "So there was no other time you felt like this? Does anything come up at all?"

The change in tone worked: the hard glint faded from Mark's eyes and he grew thoughtful again.

"Well, yeah. I guess so. I mean, you know my history with my second wife, Margery, and her holier-than-thou, richer-than-thou family. They always made me feel like I was a toad. And . . . okay, this comes up: it didn't matter how many A's I got on my report card. My dad would always say, 'Too bad you don't have any common sense. This report card and fifty cents will get you a ride on the bus. Let's see what happens when you hit the real world.' He made it pretty clear that he thought I'd fall on my face in that real world."

Mark had obviously hit a rich vein of memories and associations. "And, dammit, we *moved* so often, I never knew where I was. You have no idea how priorities changed from school to school. Once we were in a pretty decent school system and everyone was Ivy-League-bound and preppy and got status by acing academics: I turned into Mr. Super Achiever for a year. Next school I ended up in was Jock City; kids who answered questions right too often in class were nerds and usually got beaten up by this or that musclebound bully after school. So I adjusted: I joined the soccer team, kept my mouth shut in class, but kept acing papers and tests. I sort of went underground as a 'smart kid' academically—my teachers knew, but I was damned if I was going to flaunt it in front of the rest of the kids. I boned up on football and baseball and could talk jock with the best of them. Next school had a motorcycle gang. I started wearing T-shirts, stained jeans, and black boots. I was one street-smart kid in my junior year. But, damn, it was exhausting. I was certainly a chameleon—I managed to fit in pretty well at all these different places. But it was always a colossal effort at first to psych out what I thought other people expected of me. I began each of these new ventures feeling totally out of it—stupid. I had a horror of being seen as stupid. It was like the worst thing I could possibly be."

It turned out that Mark had a whole lifetime of feeling secretly "stupid," that his only way to succeed consisted of overachieving and/or pulling the wool over other people's eyes so that they wouldn't see how inadequate he really was—or felt. Julia had heard some of this before, but never in this context, and never said so passionately. She got the picture of a tiny animal running for cover. She began to *feel* how

Mark felt, spending his whole life consumed with fear, the fear of being found out as the stupid, inadequate creature he was sure he was.

And then he brought it all back up to the present. He turned on Julia: "And now what happens? You go out and have an affair. It's like everyone is doing stuff behind my back. I'm too stupid to catch on. I feel like a chump, like I said before. Sometimes it feels like you're just one more person laughing at me, the way my father laughed at me when I was a kid, saying I'd never amount to anything."

Mark was able to make a clear connection between his childhood memories and feelings and the way he felt about Julia today. Not everyone is able to make so clear a link; sometimes, at first, only the questioner will be able to see the connections. The next steps will allow you to mine those revelations to further advantage. But however much significance your partner may find in his memories, *you* will have found considerable significance, and, as you'll see, you can make use of it later on to increase your empathy.

The experience of summoning up memories is not always a pleasant one. Sometimes, as you'll see in a moment when Julia begins to explore her memories, the speaker will reach an "Aha! moment" and see his or her current situation in a new context, the context of past linked to present, and experience a pleasurable release. But just as commonly, the speaker feels upset. Remember: you're entering touchy, vulnerable territory here. Be assured that the final two steps will allow your partner to come to greater peace with this territory, however he or she may feel about opening it up initially. Mark, in fact, ended his recitation of memory feeling upset. We need to leave him in this discomfort for the moment; but you'll see that what he stirred up in himself eventually led to some important and much more pleasurable connections.

Helping Julia Reach for the Past: Where Does the "Asteroid" Come From?

In employing Step Five with Julia, Mark took his cue from the vivid image she had given him about feeling like "a lone asteroid out in space." He was still Mark, however: when he contemplated asking Julia if this image brought up anything from her past, he felt the fleeting strong impulse to defend himself against the possibility of her accusing *him* of making her feel alone. As he later told me, "I almost started out with a lecture—'I know you've felt alone, Julia, but come on, I've devoted my life to you. How could you feel alone with me?' "

However, as before, he managed to check himself, returning for a brief visit to Steps One and Two to calm himself and to detach. Another important reminder: in doing these steps, you will often find yourself returning to previous steps, generally to reinforce your detached but caring stance. In breaking down the communications process into its components, we are always in danger of presenting an artificial picture of what happens in real life. I've taken pains to show you bumps in the road, times when one or another partner resists the process of these steps and maybe even, for the moment, stops altogether, because the process is an *organic* one and will be experienced differently by different people. You'll find, through practice, as the singular arc of the steps becomes second nature to you, that you won't be conscious of what number step you're on—you'll simply return to the intent of each step as needed. Again: this is an organic and fluid process. You can speed in an instant through the first four steps ending up right away in the process of "reaching for the past" we're exploring now. Or, as I've said, you can stop with Steps One and Two, adding a little bit of Three to begin the process of hearing your partner. You can, at any point, move ahead or move back or ask for time out. While we're talking about reliable "rules" and techniques, your use of these is open to enormous choice. Eventually, you'll learn to use your instincts as a good guide of how far and how quickly to move through the steps.

But let's return to Julia: she *wanted* to make connections to her past, and did not put up any resistance to Mark's question: "When did you feel like this lone asteroid before?" She knew she had discovered fertile territory. As she later told me, "I felt so relieved to be able to talk about this stuff. I'd kept it in for so long. . . ."

Mark realized even before Julia made associations to the past that he'd hit gold with the asteroid image because of something I'd told him previously about the fifth step. Whenever your partner says something idiosyncratic about him- or herself, something that sounds like an assumption, and something that he or she might have said at any age, you've usually stumbled onto a rich lode of associations. Why? Because we learn our assumptions very early on, usually from the first messages we get from our parents. Throughout our lives, memories tend to cling to and illuminate these central assumptions: almost always, they provide a vivid understanding of the deepest messages we learned to believe about the world and ourselves. As both Mark and Julia knew, her description of herself as an "asteroid" was one of these rich routes.

"I'll tell you a really early memory," Julia said. "I was about five years old. My grandmother was living in the house and she was dying of heart disease. I didn't know she was dying at first, I just got this horrible oppressive feeling from my parents that something terrible was going on in her room. My parents were so grim about it—and they told me that I, on pain of getting spanked, was *not* to bother Grandma, ever. Unless they told me it was okay, I was not to get near her room. But I would hear my grandmother calling out. I couldn't make out the words, but something like 'Listen to me . . . come in and listen to me.' I don't know, maybe she was delirious. This was before the days that anyone had ever heard of Alzheimer's. Often my mother would be in the kitchen and my father downstairs in the basement working on something or other, both of them far away from my grandmother's room. Only I would be able to hear her calling out. But I didn't dare go in, because Mommy and Daddy told me I couldn't. Sometimes I'd run to Mommy and tell her Grandma was calling for her, but as often as not, Mommy would say not to bother her, that Grandma didn't really need anything, that she'd take care of things later. It was horrible. I can't get those faint sad whimpers out of my head.''

Julia quite naturally used the words "mommy" and "daddy" in this recounting; even her face showed the expression of a frightened little girl as she continued. "And then one day she wasn't there anymore. She had died. It was during the night; I know, because I heard muttered voices and a hospital van driving up to take her away; I didn't dare get out of bed. I knew Grandma was gone. But the horrible feeling was, if I'd only gone into her room when she was calling out, I might have been able to save her. It was my fault she died."

Julia had gone white. Tears began to run down her face. She turned to me, then to Mark. *"Now I feel like Grandma. Like I'm calling out and nobody's there to listen."* Mark was stunned into silence at first; then reached out to touch Julia's hand. "I never heard you talk about this before," he said. Julia calmed down, seemed to regain some composure.

"My parents cared so much about appearances. And about efficiency, too. When an appliance didn't work, they got rid of it that same day and replaced it. They had no use for anything that didn't *work*. I think that's what I really learned from them. That the only way to get approval or even attention from them was to be efficient, get things done correctly, work as expected. I never made this connection before, but I think that because Grandma stopped 'working,' stopped giving anything anymore, she was useless. That's the real reason my parents ignored her. I was learning something terrible about my parents. I couldn't be loved just for being me. I had to prove my worth, all the time.''

Julia made a leap to the present. She turned to Mark and abruptly asked him: ''Would you still love me if I didn't have a child?'' Something had been illuminated for her about the ambivalence she felt toward the possibility of having children. It would be more ''work'' to gain approval and a sense of worthiness. She was tired of having to produce so much and feel so little love in return. This was her ''Aha! moment,'' one that allowed her further progress in the remaining two steps. A road she never realized was there took her back to that first terrible aloneness she felt, as well as the guilt of a little girl who felt she'd killed her grandmother by ignoring her cries for help. This set up in her a deep and, until now, unconscious fear: she couldn't depend on anyone else hearing *her* cries of help either. Her only hope was to keep ''working,'' earning attention. But she was tired. She wanted to be loved without having to work so hard for it. The rewards, so far, had been so meager.

Julia ''got'' this connection as clearly as Mark had. They had constructed a whole new landscape, a whole new context in which to understand Julia's current fears, doubts, and worried expectations. As a result, they were ready to make even more connections to the present, connections that would enable them to make better sense of their relationship with each other.

But that came later. Let's stay with Step Five for a while longer, exploring, as before, different personality types' expectations.

What to Expect as You Reach for the Past
The Somatizer. We have concentrated so far on our personality types as listeners, making general points that also il-

luminate what they face as speakers. But here we need to sort out what happens when the somatizer speaks from what happens when the somatizer listens. Exploring the past is scary business for the somatizer in either case. Don't be surprised when you ask the somatizer to make associations to the past if he or she says, ''Oh, I can't begin to think about it. It gives me a headache.'' Or asthma, or arthritis, or just a general feeling of ''flu.''

Often (although not always) the somatizer is hiding memories, possibly even from him- or herself, of early physical or emotional abuse. If this is the case, even the *idea* of dredging up memories is going to be terrifying and will probably result in a return to hiding behind the usual physical complaints. You need to be patient with the somatizer, just as you need to be patient with yourself if you somatize, whether you take the questioner role or the speaker role in this step. The good news is that you usually find, over time and with practice, that the experience of putting memories into *words* is freeing. The somatizer needs to learn that *talking* is safe, that it does not equate with action, and that remembering even difficult events does not mean you have to relive them physically. This may seem obvious to the rational mind, but the emotions are not rational, and we sometimes protect ourselves from our memories because the emotional self doesn't understand that they can be looked at without harm. With luck, the somatizer has discovered by now that words won't kill him—the process of calming down, crossing the street, and listening and/or speaking in Steps Three and Four will all have paved the way for the deeper work of Step Five. Step Five is where it is for a reason: you build up to it. But expect some major resistance; be patient; keep trying; and rejoice when you once again discover, if you are a somatizer or are dealing with one, that words can't hurt you. In fact, words—when they describe memories—can lead to the deepest healing.

The Overly Cheery. We've become familiar with the fear

behind this defense: overly cheery people find it terribly threatening to stay with their own or anybody else's dark feelings. They will do anything to get out of the shadows, to emphasize the positive and "let the sun shine in." Unfortunately, however, many of the memories that surface in Step Five aren't very sunny. Expect to fight the process of the fifth step if you're overly cheery; and if you're taking the listening role, remind yourself that what your partner is recounting has to do with your *partner*. None of this need threaten you.

But the biggest reassurance the overly cheery personality needs to register is that darkness can be illuminated. Remind yourself that the whole point of this process is to shed light on everything—to *heal* wounds, to alleviate pain. The overly cheery personality can take comfort in this; the goal is what he or she has wanted to do from the start: to fix what is broken, to bring to light what has been kept in the dark. Reminding yourself of this will help whether you're the speaker or the listener. You can learn to hang on through the dark better when you know that what's coming is light.

Techniques that have worked before will work here, too: if you're the listener, remind yourself, like the somatizer, that whatever darkness comes up in your partner will not engulf you; if you're the speaker, understand that all you're saying is *words,* and that the ultimate goal is to heal whatever wounds these words may point to, not to plunge you into permanent depression. Again, it takes practice; again, your path will be made easier if you've managed to maintain the serenity and distance you've achieved in previous steps. Remember, you can always cross the street again, and again, and as many more times as it takes for you to regain your composure.

The Perfectionist. If you're a perfectionist, as a listener you will undoubtedly feel exasperated by inconsistencies in your partner's accounts of memory, particularly if you have facts about dates, places, or names to back up what you know to be the "real truth." But remember that we're not talking about real truth here; we're talking about *emotional* truth. Remember the technique that Julia used in the fourth step with Mark, the idea of hearing what he was saying as if he had prefaced it with the words: "I had a dream that . . ." This is an excellent tip to give the perfectionist: imagine that what you're hearing as your partner recounts memories are *dreams*. Indeed, there are many similarities between dreams and memories. Freud often stressed that our memories are amalgams or condensations of our earliest feelings mixed with childhood images strained through the emotional reality we're going through now. In other words, there is no "actual" documentable reality to be tested or even sought here: all you're doing is beckoning to your partner, once again, to free-associate, but this time using whatever images come up that are connected with his or her past. Suspend disbelief; pretend you're at an avant garde play where anything is allowed to happen.

Similarly, if you're the speaker, allow your imagination more free rein. Try to fight your editing urges: if something doesn't click rationally, but it's what you can't help feeling emotionally, stay with the emotion. You're not after a footnoted document of your life; you're after *feelings* about your past, and whatever images or events or remembered voices elicit those feelings. This can be especially difficult for perfectionists for another reason: they are often wed to *one* picture, and one picture only, of certain people and events. For example, one perfectionist client of mine has a hard time allowing himself to see his parents as anything but perfect. He suppresses any negative feelings about them, because his "rational" mind tells him they paid for his college education, worked hard, sacrificed, and in general were beyond reproach. The problem was, he kept having intrusive feelings of resentment toward them that didn't square with the image his conscious mind strove so assiduously to protect. In the course of fifth-step work, as he became convinced that the object was to explore his *feelings* (not "reality"), he was slowly able to tug out memories of his parents that weren't so golden. He fought them, but slowly revealed them. And the result was an immense relief.

In fact, as we've seen in every other step, perfectionists generally find, whether as speakers or listeners, tremendous relief in giving themselves permission to occupy the freer, more dreamlike state asked of them in these steps, including Step Five. When you feel you don't *have* to take the stance of belligerent interrogator and efficient footnoter, when you've relaxed your hold on "the facts," you generally end up heaving a long, grateful sigh.

The Blamer. The blamer, whether as speaker or listener, feels he can't survive revealing one terrible and secret truth about himself: if he tells everything about his past, he'll make it clear that *he* is to blame for all of it. Again, we tend to project our fears outward when we feel too threatened to "own" them. Blamers blame generally because, secretly (and usually unconsciously), they're certain of their own guilt.

The task, then, for blamers, is always to remind themselves that reality is complex and problems are not solved by pointing fingers. It helps blamers to think of the exploration of the past called for in Step Five as a kind of emotional inventory-taking: all they're doing is looking for new data to make the picture fuller and clearer. This attitude will help them both as speakers and listeners. Understand that, as the past is revealed (either by you or by your partner), you're going to feel a nearly overwhelming desire to pull whatever you say or hear into a blaming scenario: "Of course, if your mother hadn't remarried, none of this would have happened" or "If my father had taken care of the family as he should have, I would have turned out differently." But understand that you can resist this temptation. Suspend judgment. Remind yourself that all you're after is a fuller inventory of emotion. You don't need to justify anyone's actions, including your own. Again, when blamers do manage to suspend their blaming urges, they often feel an unaccustomed relief. A good mantra for blamers might simply be "Everything is not his fault. We are all part of a larger picture." Repeat that to yourself when the tidal wave of blame seems ready to build and break.

The Advice-Giver. Poor advice-givers! In asking them to do these steps, it will always seem as if we're holding them back from expressing their love, their wisdom, their ability to fix things, to help, to heal. The conscious motive for most advice-givers, as we've seen, is that *they* know the answer and if we'll only just pay heed to it, we'll fix our lives.

This means that, as speakers, advice-givers usually dismiss their own problems: if they can't "fix" a memory, why bring it up? As a result, they generally have very limited childhood memories, and are unused to reaching for the past. They share the overly cheery personality's fear of staying too long with dark, ambiguous, or anxiety-provoking feelings. As listeners, their problem is even more obvious. How can they hold back from giving their helpful opinions?

Advice-givers are commonly driven by a deep and unconscious fear of being abandoned. The motive to give advice is often to make sure the rest of the world does what it's supposed to, acts in predictable and approved-of ways, and *stays with the advice-giver.* This is particularly the case in the advice-giver's intimate relationships. "I'm so afraid you'll fall down and skin your knee, then it'll get infected" or "If you don't look where you're going, you'll get hit by a car" or "If you don't take care of your cold, it will turn into pneumonia. . . ." These worried expressions of concern often hide the fear that the loved one will leave, change the world for the worse, even die.

As a listener, the advice-giver needs to allow the speaker to fall down and skin his knee, to tolerate the other's "mistakes," to let go of other people's behavior. It is hoped that through the first four steps, the advice-giver will have learned to tolerate risk more easily, and thus to tolerate the information he or she is given by the speaker—and in general be more disposed to listening to someone else's memories without rushing to interpret or "fix" them.

Advice-givers face an even greater challenge when they're the speakers: it will probably take a good deal of time before they can allow their evanescent memories to take more definite form. Be patient with the advice-giver; be patient with yourself if you are one. Learn that you can survive some risk-taking. Remind yourself, as our other personality types have been asked to remind themselves, that all you're doing is coming up with, or listening to, *words*. When you attempt to investigate your past and you feel blocked, gently repeat this question to yourself: "What are the things I'm leaving out?" Eventually, more memories will surface. Even if you don't understand all of them at first, even if you only get half a memory, or an isolated image or voice that you can't connect with anything else, allow it to surface and acknowledge it. After a while you'll relax, more memories will connect, and you'll see that, for all its ambiguity, the world is a less threatening place than you thought it was.

The Moralist. As listeners, moralists need to guard against such interventions as "How could you be so childish to dwell on *that?*" Moralists attempt to live in black-and-white worlds. People, especially people in memory, tend to be seen as archetypes, not unlike the cutout characters in old medieval morality plays. One character is "Envy," another "Jealousy," another "Greed." Other characters are "Mercy," "Charity," "Honesty." To some extent, these godlike creatures inhabit all of our earliest memories, especially those of our parents. When we were infants, parents *were* gods: larger, infinitely more powerful than we, creatures on whom we depended for our very lives. But the moralist frequently takes this larger-than-life view of human beings to heart; his whole present world is saturated with it. You are "right" or you are "wrong." Moralists feel the urge to reduce people to preconceived ideas, make them fit forms with which they are familiar and comfortable. What they don't feel comfortable with is "complex reality."

Unfortunately, what comes up in our memories is almost always complex—ambiguous, hard to pin down, susceptible to more than one interpretation. We've seen before that moralists gain from the idea that the process of exploration they undergo in these steps serves a greater good: by letting go of as many preconceptions and fiercely held beliefs as possible—at least for the moment—we stand to get the greatest possible clarity about our partners and ourselves.

As with perfectionists, whether as speakers or listeners, moralists need to guard against their urge to edit out anything that does not fit their moral scheme of things. The best possible exercise for moralists is to practice free association. When images and memories begin to come to you unbidden, when you allow yourself to begin to express them exactly as they occur to you, you have triumphed. Moralists can practice this alone to get used to the freedom asked of them in the fifth step. When they see that their moral world doesn't come crumbling down, that they're not after all inviting the "Devil" to take over, they are more able to let up on themselves when they speak or listen to their partners.

As always, have patience. Remember that you're fighting lifelong resistances. Any ability to free-associate, and share that free association with your partner, or tolerate it when your partner shares with you, is progress—and reason to celebrate.

You have a vivid landscape open to you by the end of Step Five. Connections have been made that you probably never realized were there. The jigsaw puzzle has some crucial pieces in place: the overall picture begins to emerge. More important, you have the comfort of realizing that much—perhaps even all—of what you and your partner are complaining about in each other has unmistakable roots in both your pasts. In fact, a lot of what's bothering you has nothing to do with your partner at all, but rather with assumptions each of you learned years before you met each other. It is a psychological truism that we act out primal family dramas with our love partners: now you know, more clearly, what some of those dramas are.

Where do we go from here? Are there more ways we can connect? How do we move from past to present? How do we make use of the rich data we've managed to uncover?

Step Six will lead us further: read on.

STEP SIX

EMPATHIZING THROUGH DETACHMENT

STEP SIX, "EMPATHIZING THROUGH DETACHMENT," means stepping back for a moment to review all your partner has said to you, allowing yourself to see the world through his or her eyes as completely as you can.

Our task throughout these steps has been to set the stage for what the philosopher Martin Buber called an I/thou relationship. Although Buber used this term for man's fuller relationship to a higher spiritual power, we think it fits for loved ones. This is a stance in which you experience your partner's full complexity: as whole and round a being as you know yourself to be. The reason you've been giving your partner center stage from Step One on has been to see and understand your partner in his or her own terms. The sixth step now celebrates and affirms what you've learned about your partner, the speaker—the "thou" in the I/thou relationship. (Later on, the seventh step will unite you—"I"—with that "thou.") The sixth step encourages you to affirm your *love* for your partner, and to focus on the things that you share and that connect you.

It is also a silent step. In an interior monologue, you put together all the data you've received from listening to your partner and permit yourself, as deeply as possible, to *feel* what your partner has communicated to you about his or her own feelings.

This does not mean that you cross back from the side of the street you've been on since Step Two. Detachment here is as important as empathy. The sixth step depends upon your ability to maintain two seemingly paradoxical stances: objectivity and deep caring. But you've been building up to this all along; Step Six is an intensification of the kind of caring objectivity you've been cultivating from the start. Not that you won't be tempted to imagine that all barriers have disappeared: the desire to believe that you can simply "merge" after all the difficult territory you've covered in the preceding steps will be, for many listeners, hard to resist. But remember that even during this empathic step, you are still two different people.

But let's not underplay the "love" or "empathy" part of Step Six. The objective stance you took in Steps One and Two—recognizing tension and crossing the street—along with the kind of close inner, outer, and historical listening you've employed in Steps Three, Four, and Five, have a double payoff: not only have you achieved more objectivity about your partner (partly by not taking what he or she says so hurtfully to heart), but you are also in a position to empathize in a much fuller and more productive way. If you've gotten this far with your partner, you're probably glad you've made the journey. You've more than likely felt stirrings of an emotion that was long dormant when you began: *love.* In fact, you wouldn't be expending this kind of effort to hear your partner if love weren't a very big motivation.

The data you get from listening via the process we're outlining is tremendously rich. As we've seen, it can revolutionize your and your partner's perceptions of what is really being said, what is truly going on in his or her heart and mind. By now you've discovered a good deal about how the past intrudes on the present—how rooted certain patterns can be. You've explored certain hidden meanings in your partner's words and behavior. In Step Six, you can identify with your partner in a particularly clear and productive way, acknowledging to yourself that you have felt similar feelings. You're building a concrete understanding of how your partner feels by empathizing in this objective, but nonetheless heartfelt, way.

Not All Endings Are Happy

As you've discovered by now, true communication is hard and sometimes frightening work. Intimacy takes courage. When you begin to uncover patterns from the past, you can never predict exactly how they will affect the relationship you are in today. That's the risk both partners must be willing to take, even if they mutually conclude that their discoveries mean they should split up. Sometimes you get to some bedrock differences that neither partner is willing to accept. However, even if separation becomes inevitable, taking careful time to reach such a decision can do a lot to ameliorate the most destructive forms of hostility. Through intimate listening, both partners feel they have participated in the decision. They have mutually come to the understanding that, at the present time, they are better off apart. Taking separate paths is more strengthening and constructive than continuing together.

Indeed, sometimes the hidden meanings in seemingly "minor" differences reveal fundamentally insoluble conflicts. But even if this process of intimate communication reveals that you and your partner can no longer stay together, it becomes possible to experience other emotions besides feeling attacked by your partner. Again, you're both working together at this process of self-discovery; neither one of you is left out. You can end up truly wanting the best for each other, even if it means splitting up. This isn't to say that irrational rage during the process of divorce (if divorce is what you pursue) won't arise, even if you employ all of our intimate listening steps; it's perfectly normal to feel angry as you go through the process of ending a love relationship. In fact, anger is often a necessary condition for achieving separation. But it becomes much more manageable if it happens in the context of the intimate communication and listening channels that you and your partner can learn to open up between you.

However, in my experience it's more common for a committed couple to find new ways to increase and enjoy their togetherness. In fact, if you've made it to Step Six—which, as I've said, is the "love" step—you've more than likely proved to each other that you *do* want to stay together. The sixth step, once you've reached it, usually announces that you're just about home free. Although your partner is still occupying center stage in Step Six (don't worry, you'll have your say in Step Seven), you are now able, strongly and unmistakably, to link your heart with your partner's heart.

Because we're beginning to explore "love" head-on, with all its mystical intangibilities, it's difficult to talk about the effects of this step in the abstract. So let's concentrate on some real-life experience of it. Mark and Julia, as usual, will be our first instructors. Then the rest of our personality types will, also as usual, shed even more light on what it means to empathize through detachment.

Two Asteroids, Not One: Julia "Meets" Mark for the First Time

Julia's "sixth-step moment about Mark," as she later described it to me, had some very clear imagery. "I'd heard so much from Mark, and by now I was able to *see* certain strong themes. I stress the word 'see' because I did actually see Mark in my mind as the baby I'd conjured up back in . . . I guess it was the fourth step, where I let my mind free-associate." You'll remember that Julia described Mark when she did this step as "a cranky, abandoned baby in a crib, howling in frustration and sadness and fear'' and, later, ''crawling down a path, crying, lost, with other cruel kids looking on from the sidelines, jeering at him.''

Then she said she let that baby grow up for an instant, remembering what Mark had told her about his first two marriages, the college-sweetheart sham of a marriage that had ended up leaving him feeling inadequate, the second marriage to Margery, which also left him feeling ''less than.'' She flashed back to his description of all the chameleon changes he'd had to make, moving from town to town, trying to be a jock here, a biker there, an intellectual genius someplace else. She was haunted by his father's dismissal of Mark, how he'd told Mark that he'd never amount to anything in ''the real world.'' She saw, with less judgment and more understanding, the paradox of Mark: how he unwittingly set himself up to be disappointed, all the while trying to convey a supercompetent image. She understood more about his stance of martyrdom at work, how it allowed him to feel superior as well as be an object of sympathy. She colored this with what she knew about him emotionally—how difficult it was to keep himself contained, how afraid he was of his own feelings, reacting to them as if they were toxic and had to be gotten rid of as soon as possible. And somehow, as she reflected on all of this, she began to feel—more deeply and with greater force than she'd felt before—how her affair must have wounded him, how devastating it must have been to him. His feelings of self-worth were hacked at the root by it; it was just one more traumatic bit of evidence to add to a lifetime of evidence that he was *not enough*. He couldn't make her, or anyone else, truly happy. She'd seen through him, and she'd turned to somebody else for what he couldn't give her. She saw how strong his own impulsiveness was in the face of this terrible feeling of inadequacy: her upcoming business trip threatened to be, she realized, the final trigger for Mark. Feeling abandoned once again, he was afraid *he* would turn to somebody else.

"It was as if these thoughts, memories, feelings, pictures were all simultaneous," Julia said. "It was like a patchwork quilt taking shape in front of my eyes. At first it was only Mark I saw; this amalgam of information he'd given me seemed to 'create' him as a baby and a teenager and a young man and the man I knew him to be, all at once, like photographic images superimposed over each other. But then, when I allowed myself really to feel how alone he felt, I saw a connection to me. I entered the picture in my mind, walking in shyly almost, extending my hand, then my arms, to him. I felt, for that moment, the incredibly strong urge to touch him, hold him, let him know that I understood his aloneness. As dissimilar as our backgrounds and emotional makeups were, the effect on us wasn't so different. In a second, it was as if I could fit myself into most of his feelings like a foot into the right-size shoe. I knew, for this moment—really *knew*—how he felt. I felt, in some way, like I was meeting him for the first time. And it unleashed such a flood of compassion in me. Compassion and . . . love."

Julia also realized that she'd lost most of her own defensiveness: in the fullness of the "sixth-step moment," she felt she could see Mark more clearly and with more love and compassion; as she "entered" the picture, she had a fleeting but strong feeling of compassion for herself. "This was a kind of subsidiary thing," Julia said. "But the woman who approached Mark with her arms open in my mind's eye was also the grown-up little girl who'd felt guilty for 'killing' her grandmother. I can't describe it, but my acceptance of Mark was also somehow an acceptance and a forgiveness of myself. I saw us in all of our separate fear and pain, and experienced a kind of cleansing love and compassion for both of us."

Julia, Transformed: Mark's Sixth-Step Moment

Mark had a sixth-step experience that was in some ways similar to Julia's but also had several important differences. "I saw myself in Julia, identified with her feelings, when I went over what she had told me; but I also saw myself in *contrast* to what she said. It was like, as I began to get a clearer picture of her, I saw what made us different as well as what made us the same."

As Mark reviewed what Julia had told him, it was, however, predictably difficult for him to stay quiet about it. "Every time I had the glimmer of a revelation, I wanted to tell her about it. I felt like a kid who'd stumbled onto the right answer to a complicated algebra question and couldn't keep it to himself—I wanted to shout it out to the teacher!" But Mark had learned enough about his own impulsiveness to keep himself in check. "I'd already learned in the first five steps that I won't explode if I keep a feeling to myself, at least for a few moments. Anyway, I knew that I could talk in the seventh step, so I kept that as an inducement to keep quiet during this sixth-step business."

This "sixth-step business" revealed a complicated whole picture of Julia: "That image of the asteroid kept things in focus for me," Mark said. "It was such a clear picture of cold aloneness, and I understood it in my gut. But I also saw that little girl who thought she was responsible for her grandmother's death—and the little girl who felt pressured to get things right, to keep working so that she'd be useful to somebody, whose whole purpose, she thought, was to 'deliver the goods' to somebody. I know Julia's parents and they really are nice people, but they sit on the edge of their seats and feel guilty if they aren't planning their next productive step. Vacations for them are out of the question. Then I flashed on Julia as she was when I first met her, when I was still married to

Margery. I can't tell you what a wicked gleam she had in her eye—she was so full of passion and daring. It was like, for that moment, she could let out this really mischievous, dangerous spirit, one that was incredibly captivating. I fell in love with that spirit. And I could put together from what Julia said that she loved—and missed—that spirit in herself, too.

"So many pieces of the puzzle fell into place. I remembered how she brought in having a child. It's a difficult area for both of us. I mean, it isn't the first time I realized we were torn about it. But I flashed back onto her words: 'I don't have a clue if I even want to have a child. I just feel burdened, like we're supposed to be starting a family because that's what the rules are. But what are the rules? What is it we're supposed to be doing? What am I supposed to be doing?' I felt her confusion in my gut, and it mirrored my own. And then I had that picture of a cyclone, and the debris left by it, and Julia walking through the wreckage, dazed, not knowing where she was or what was required of her. And I felt that fear and burden like they were my own, too. I remembered how she said she wanted so much to hear from me on the phone when she went away to Chicago—'Please, please, just *hear* me. *Be* there,' she'd said. 'Don't judge me. Just be there.' And, although it was still horribly painful for me, I was able for that moment to understand why she'd reached out for 'contact' when she had that affair. Her feelings of being out of contact had just become intolerable. She had to make contact with something, somebody, anybody. . . ."

Mark repeated that by creating this larger, fuller picture of Julia, he gained the ability to identify with her feelings of aloneness and to appreciate their emotional differences. "I could understand better why Julia shuts down, why she retreats into herself and pulls the lid over her feelings. I didn't feel so threatened anymore by that impulse in her. I saw that it was just a different way of handling stress than I used. I guess, for the first time, I saw the contrast between us without judging it. Always before, I'd felt superior to her, like I was so much more capable of 'emotional honesty' than she was. But now I know we just have different styles of retreat. Mine is to explode, hers is to shut down.''

Mark also said that while he still felt wounded by Julia's affair, the pain had lost some of its sharpness; it had become more distant. ''I guess really listening to Julia meant I couldn't blame her so easily. I learned a simple lesson about her, about me, about any human being: *We do things for reasons.* We react to pressure, from within ourselves, from the outside world, in ways that we've learned will relieve that pressure best.'' This wasn't just a surface understanding, Mark said. ''As I realized in the fourth step, I was learning that I could do more than 'snorkel'—I could deep-sea dive, survive going deeper into my feelings than I used to think I could. How could I dismiss Julia so easily? How could I dismiss *myself* so easily anymore? I'd discovered—actually *re*discovered—something remarkable. I loved Julia. I wanted us to be able to be with each other again without that horrible, sickening pain of feeling alone, misunderstood. I realized now that I wasn't the only one who suffered that pain. Julia felt it, in her way, just as much as I ever had.''

It's important to stress here that, without love, Mark and Julia's experience of the sixth step—in the unlikely event that they were able even to reach it—would have been profoundly different. We are, in Step Six, at that core place of a love relationship, the furnace that fuels marriage—whose fuel is, in fact, love. Without that fuel there's little hope. If Mark hadn't been able to connect to his feelings of love for Julia, he might simply have seen her as a conniving, cold, cheating WASP who had a lousy childhood. Similarly, without love, Julia might have seen Mark as a hotheaded, childish underachiever who never got over *his* lousy childhood. In fact, they were ready to come up with negative summations like these before they embarked on these steps. Immersed in their own defensiveness and pain, they had kept themselves far away from their respective furnaces of love, which might have warmed and softened their views of each other. It was easier in this pained, defensive state to attack, blame, lash out against the "enemy" and then withdraw to protect yourself. Whatever love there was, was deeply buried. It took work to find it, to be warmed by it again.

Much of what these steps are meant to do is reconnect you to your own capacity for love, to remind you that there *is* a furnace burning away down beneath the cold layers of defense and fear and pain. Love is the animating force of all these steps; the sixth step enables you to make full contact with it.

But now, let's go back to our old friends the personality types for more evidence of how to locate, tolerate, and even learn to enjoy the warmth of love in Step Six.

How Different Personalities Can Learn to Enjoy Love

The Somatizer. Whether listeners or speakers, if somatizers have managed to make it to the sixth step, to tolerate their feelings as well as those of their partners, they have the chance of a wonderful reward. But first, if you're a somatizer, congratulate yourself for having gotten here. You've proved to yourself once again that you can survive without the protective covering of an earache, asthma, migraine, arthritis, or a sudden mysterious onset of "flu."

When you somatize you are acting at a very primal level, using defenses you probably learned in your earliest childhood. When defenses are rooted this deep, you will quite naturally feel enormous resistance to giving them up. Unconsciously, you're convinced that they are your secrets of survival, which they may well have been back then. I've stressed in every discussion of this category the need to go slowly, to expect "relapse," to congratulate yourself for every moment of progress, each time you're able to tolerate your own feelings without resorting to the cover-up of physical distress. You've jumped light years by getting to the sixth step; it is a tremendously healing step for you, because it is, in a sense, the payoff you never dared to believe you might receive. By staying with your partner, you've begun to make contact with a very pleasurable feeling of empathy, of love, of understanding. The thing you feared most—emotional honesty—turns out to have been the one key you needed to get to this blissful state.

You may be so happy to have reached "connection" in Step Six, however, that we need to remind you, gently, that you haven't in fact "merged" completely with your partner. What you've discovered is your *love* for your partner. On some level, we all want to "merge;" forgive yourself for that universal desire. But discovering that you can truly empathize with another human being, that you truly feel love for another separate being, is just as good, maybe even better. The main thing is: *Rejoice that you've come this far.* You're a pioneer. You've probably never been here before.

The Overly Cheery. The sixth step is payoff time for the overly cheery person, too, whether as listener or speaker. Terrified of being in a depression, whether their own or their partners' (which on some level they think they must make their own), overly cheery people have undoubtedly mistrusted every step in this process. Each movement toward emotional honesty seemed to beckon to all the dark dungeons and dragons of the psyche: the route will have seemed fraught with danger. But now, in the sixth step, as you allow yourself to empathize with your partner, or permit your partner to empathize with you, you're experiencing a positive frame of mind that is genuine, that you have *earned.* The love you feel has not only sprung from your "nice" or "light" feelings but also proceeds from your darker fears, your more troubling emotions. You've proved, like the somatizer, that you can survive these feelings: you don't have to cut them off prematurely. You've navigated your way through a dark night of the soul. The nature of the "pleasure" you now feel is richer, deeper, more rooted, less fearful than it is likely you've ever experienced before. It comes from a full, free acceptance of who you are, who your partner is. You've ended up more satisfying where you wanted to go all along: to feelings of real love, real empathy.

The Perfectionist. Perfectionists have a peculiar dilemma in the sixth step: here, finally, is what they've been after all along—a perfect moment. The dilemma comes in realizing how they *got* to the perfect moment. This connection of empathy, this recognition of another person's feelings, this ability to identify with and feel love for the other person all have come as the result of surrendering control, forgetting about "the facts," allowing the other person to emerge freely and without contradiction or correction. All of this has come from using tactics opposite to those you've always used before. But the rewards are unaccountably great. By giving up the impulse to count the trees, you've begun to see the forest.

The means of getting here are unnervingly new to the perfectionist, but as with previous steps, the experience of employing these means is ultimately colored by a huge relief. Like the overly cheery, perfectionists who finally get what they want feel more satisfied than they could have predicted. This perfect moment of love and empathy and understanding is rounder, richer, with more ambiguity and shadow than they are used to seeing or tolerating. That they could love something or someone "flawed" is a profoundly new concept. It turns out that those "flaws" weren't the massive intolerable cracks perfectionists once thought they were. Accepting a partner's inconsistencies also means accepting the perfectionist's own inconsistencies. Love for a partner can also spill over into love for yourself.

The Blamer. An intense feeling of guilt has plagued you all along if you're a blamer; it's been all you can do to keep it at bay throughout these steps. But what you reach when you experience Step Six is an unaccustomed feeling of release from your own self-absorption. Feeling empathy for other people means truly recognizing that they're *there:* they're not just some mirror reflecting back aspects of you that you'd rather not see. The feeling of "It's all my fault" that you usually transmute into "It's all *your* fault" has, by the sixth step, finally abated. One blaming client of mine told me that, in the sixth step, he became aware of how much anxiety he normally was in because now, for this moment, it had disappeared. "It's like I was in this awful, painful hangover all the time that I thought was normal. When it lifted, I couldn't believe life could be like that. Not this terrible pressure all the time to look out for who was doing what to whom, to look around for someone to point the finger at. It's like some vise had released its grip on my head—and my forehead, my shoulders, my back—and it all, in one downward movement, *relaxed.*" He let out a long, slow sigh; his relief was palpable. "All this and a feeling of love for my wife, too? How did that happen?"

Sometimes the experience of the sixth step can be so unnerving to the blamer that he or she may need to "exit" for a moment and get used to this new feeling of softness and relief—meditate, enjoy the moment, accept it, and entertain a new notion: Life *doesn't* have to be a sharp-edged grind—you don't have to constantly look behind you for the next stab in the back.

The Advice-Giver. In the sixth step, advice-givers finally have changed their dynamic of acting as their partners' parents to one of seeing themselves as their partners' peers. This is a fearful business. As we've seen in previous explorations of this personality, the advice-giver's most powerful (if usually unconscious) fear is of being abandoned. Worried expressions of concern for a loved one's health and well-being are covers for the fear that the loved one will leave or die. But the advice-giver also has a hard time accepting another person's power. By "taking over," the advice-giver feels in control; it's a way of dominating people whose power they're afraid of. The amazing news usually gotten to in the sixth step is that people will stay even if they're allowed to wield their own power to go. They don't have to be manipulated, controlled, overseen.

Another secret fear of the advice-giver is that unless love is expressed continually—in the form of controlling advice—loved ones won't realize that you love them. The notion of expressing your love by *listening* is a very difficult one for the advice-giver. But by now, in the sixth step, you have abundant evidence that this is so. Letting go of control is sometimes the best way to keep love.

The Moralist. We said about the somatizer that the urge to somatize probably goes back to earliest childhood. Actually, all of the obstacle courses we set for ourselves, all of the defenses we cling to and that we're exploring in these personality types, are deeply rooted in early life experience and are there because we were once convinced we needed them to survive.

One moralist client of mine, whose father was an alcoholic and whose mother was a "long-suffering" schoolteacher, particularly illustrates this: "I always had the feeling I had to choose between my 'bad' dad and my 'good' mom," this woman says today. "My dad, when he was drunk, would sometimes get really sloppy and self-pitying and tell me what a wonderful, misunderstood, sensitive guy he really was, and that the whole problem was my uptight mother who wouldn't accept him for what he was. I knew even then—I remember being about nine years old—that this wasn't the kind of stuff a daddy was supposed to be telling his daughter, but I felt for him. Then, when he'd turn belligerent, break a window, slam a door, leave to go out to the bar again, my mother would launch into what a horrible, unfeeling, irresponsible man he was, and how, thank God, I took after my mother's side of the family, because if I'd been like my father, I would be doomed. I felt like a piece of meat torn at by two hungry dogs—pulled this way, pulled that way. And I know that when I get self-righteous with my husband, berating him for his irresponsibility, I'm sounding like my mother, and sort of defending myself against ever being like my father. The secret is, I was always jealous of Dad being able to storm out of the house and get away. That made me hate him more—and envy him more."

In doing these steps with her husband, especially in the open territory of the sixth step, this woman finally has been able to experience the relief of not having to decide between the "good mom" and the "bad dad." "That's not the point of doing these steps, to choose like that," she says. "When I realize I don't have to see myself in this old tug-of-war between good and bad, that the whole idea behind these steps is to be more open and understand more clearly, to connect with my husband's feelings rather than to judge them, it seems unbelievable that I'm *allowed* to do that!" The first time she got to the sixth step, she cried. "It was like I was allowing myself to love my husband, like I didn't have to *defend* myself against loving him. And for me, that was like allowing myself to love my 'bad' dad. I discovered, through listening to my husband, that things weren't always one way or the other. There were more sides to reality than I'd been able to see before. And to feel *love* as the result of looking more freely at my husband, well, that seemed too good to be true."

One definition of good mental health is the ability to tolerate ambiguity, ambivalence, paradox. We've been learning in all of these steps, but perhaps most poignantly in Step Six, to accept one of the most striking paradoxes of all: to be able to empathize, you need to maintain distance. To be able to connect, you need to know where your boundaries are.

The urge to merge, to suckle at the mother's breast, to lose all sense of boundary between you and your loved one is tremendously strong in all of us. Some of us flee to feeling states that appear to promise this merging: witness the overly cheery and the advice-givers, who concentrate on the positive, or who rush in to "fix" you so that they can dismiss all possibility of dissonance, of separateness. Some of us defend ourselves with all our energy against merging, because we were, usually at some distant crucial state in our pasts, disappointed so badly by not being able to make contact: somatizers, perfectionists, blamers, and moralists are all examples of these. The ability to tolerate feelings that confuse you and threaten your ability to *stay with them* and maintain a caring distance is not easily acquired. But when you manage to acquire it, you discover, as all the people we've talked about in this book have discovered, that you *can* make satisfying contact with your partner. You uncover the source of love in you, and its inexhaustibility. You discover that you don't have to defend yourself so vigilantly against feelings. You find out that your partner is made of the same emotional stuff that you are made of. Your partner longs for contact just as you do; your partner is afraid of being abandoned and rejected and hurt, just as you are.

The sixth step provides an incredibly healing balm; here you find out that love *is* possible, you *can* feel it, you *can* tolerate someone else's expression of it, you *can* express it yourself. What more do we need than this? Why, in fact, isn't Step Six the last one in the series?

By now you can see your partner clearly; if you're lucky, you realize that, even with all his or her conflicting feelings and experiences and fears laid bare, you *love* your partner. But you need to go further. The spotlight all along has been on your partner. Now you have to walk into the light, too.

That's what Step Seven is all about.

STEP SEVEN

BUILDING A BRIDGE

STEP SEVEN, "BUILDING A BRIDGE," means telling your partner what you want to say, using your partner's language. You've become acutely aware of the "thou" half of the "I/thou" relationship: you now know much more about your partner's feelings and emotional context, what his or her words really mean. Now it's time to give your partner just as rich a sense of the "I" half, how *you* feel, using terms that he or she will understand.

This means learning to reframe your thinking as a result of listening to your partner, making analogies to what he or she has said, emphasizing the connections between you so that your partner can begin to understand your point of view as clearly and empathically as possible. You're no longer talking out of defensiveness: you now perceive both of you as two emotionally whole and complicated human beings who can communicate with each other freely, out of strength, not out of an urge to lash out or withdraw. In other words, this time you're in contact as equals. You're now able to say what *you* are feeling in the best, most complete way, because you know how to speak to your partner in language he or she will be able to absorb.

As you'll see from Julia and Mark's experience, this can be an amazingly rewarding experience. You may even feel, for the moment, that you and your partner have permanently transcended all obstacles to communication: you're now home free. Alas, it's virtually assured that once you've completed the seven steps, you will regress (possibly very quickly) to old vengeful or defensive tactics. Why? Because freedom and clarity can be hard to adjust to. It's likely that you and your partner will feel strange in this new connection to each other; it may take some time getting used to the idea that you really *can* share the same language and treat each other as equals. You may feel discomfort with this new closeness for another subliminal reason. Unconsciously, you may not want to allow this "stranger" (who is not a member of your childhood family) *in* so completely. The closeness to your partner may feel good, but it may also feel disloyal—dislodging, as you may feel you are, your original family with an "outsider." It may take some time and practice to accept intimacy between you and your partner as permissible.

The main point is that your progress will probably be rocky. Life is a series of fits and starts, progressions followed by regressions: success and defeat are a part of the nature of growth. Moving forward is almost always followed by moving back—before you move forward again. Over time, as you learn to re-create the connection between you again and again, you'll learn to tolerate the success of reaching each other as well as the defeat, sometimes, of not being able to get all the way across the "bridge."

However, Step Seven teaches you and your partner something you can never unlearn: that it is possible to speak to and hear each other with love and clarity; that it is possible, truly, to *connect.* And there's another dividend: once across the bridge, you generally find that a solution to whatever problem initially caused friction between you and your partner will have suggested *itself.* We've concentrated purely on listening in these steps, not on "action," because it is through listening that a creative, constructive course of action is revealed. Acting before you know how you feel or how your partner feels is almost always a mistake. Action is most constructive when it is allowed to grow out of an organic process of understanding.

But let's allow Julia and Mark to show you this themselves.

Julia to Mark: "Please Be a Friendly Voice"

Mark looked different to Julia as she began to speak in the seventh step. "He looked softer, more childlike," Julia told me later, "so much more vulnerable. I had never felt such understanding of his neediness before, or felt less like judging that neediness as immature or overbearing. And somehow, accepting Mark this way also meant accepting more of my own pain and aloneness."

Julia said to Mark: "I'm afraid of going away, but I know, if we stay in regular contact on the phone, it will help so much. But please don't argue with me when we speak— please let's make our communication as warm and positive as we can. Whenever we argue, but especially on the phone, it makes me feel totally out of contact with you and, worse, out of contact with myself. I shut down like a zombie. So, if you promise not to argue, I promise you I won't break off contact or detach from you. I understand now that I have often shut down with you before, and how much pain that causes you. I promise, on this trip, to tell you what I'm feeling, to be clear about what I'm doing every day, and not to lie. I will keep as much distance as possible between me and Charles. If I have to talk to him, I will tell you about it. But mostly I will let you know I love you and miss you." Julia had been looking into Mark's eyes all this time. Now she sighed, closed her eyes for a moment, and looked at him again: "You always ask me what I dreamed about the night before, and I always cut you off. I know you want to know about what's going on inside me. Well, it might be hard, but I've decided to keep a dream journal to capture whatever I remember each morning I'm away, and I'll tell you about those dreams. I want you to know more."

Julia paused again, her voice softer when she continued: "I know I can't make you trust me. I know I have to earn that trust. And I know, sometimes, when I feel like a criminal, it's not even that you've made me feel that way—it's just how I think of myself. I accept that as a problem I've got to deal with. But I love you, and I want us to connect. Please be a friendly voice when I talk to you. . . ."

By addressing Mark's greatest fears—how she'd handle meeting Charles, how she would manage to keep in regular touch with Mark while she was away—Julia was speaking his language. Offering to keep a dream journal was a special reaching-out: she was making it clear to Mark that she was serious about letting him in as deeply as she could. By demonstrating her receptivity to Mark's needs and her desire to meet them, she could make her own needs known and heard. By speaking Mark's "language," she could reveal something essential about herself. And she discovered something interesting about the concessions she had agreed to make: "I don't feel like these are onerous obligations," Julia said. "I actually *want* to let Mark in more. I ant to be able to talk to him at regular intervals while I'm away. I even want to keep a dream journal! There's no sense of white-knuckling it here: for some reason, stuff I couldn't imagine doing before without groaning I now look forward to eagerly."

Julia's recognition that her "concessions" weren't really concessions at all; that what she was creating with Mark wasn't a series of compromises but rather plans they were making together out of equal desire, is important. These steps are not designed to enable you to "settle" for something you don't truly want. Compromise is not the goal. What we're enabling you to do here is locate a genuine *desire* to connect with your partner, so that whatever you work out together proceeds from *truly wanting to do it*. This is the aim of "building a bridge": creating a connection between your true desires and your partner's true desires. This is something you *want* to do; not something you feel you *have* to do. More than likely, once you've come to the kind of deep understanding the previous steps have afforded you, this "desire" to connect won't be something you'll have to search for. It will be there already—in fact, it will be one of the strongest urges you feel.

Mark to Julia: "Please Hear My Neediness"

Mark began by admitting to Julia that he knew his neediness could get out of hand: "I know I get paranoid, I know I just expect that people are doing stuff to me behind my back, that they're talking about me, laughing at me. And I believe you now, that you want to be honest with me, that you love me, care about me. I also know that you tend to shut down when I get really anxious—I understand much more about what's happening when you do that, and I don't take it so personally anymore. I'll try not to express my neediness, when I feel it, so urgently—like it's something *you* have to fix right then and there, like it's your fault. I know it's not your fault. I know I have to take care of my feelings of emptiness myself. I'll really try not to lay that responsibility on you anymore."

Mark now paused, cleared his throat, and continued almost in a whisper: "But please be there for *me,* too. Know that this trip is very stressful for me. Know that just the thought of you going to see that guy again makes my blood boil. Know that I'm trying with all my might to control my temper, to control these explosive feelings. I *will* be that friendly voice when we talk, I promise. I *want* to be that friendly voice. Thank you for agreeing to talk with me several times a day. Let's make a schedule of phone dates that we really keep. And I'll keep myself from going into my usual paranoid mode. And . . . oh yeah"—Mark laughed a little—"the practical stuff. You know how I resist working on the house, especially when you're away. I have to say I'm a little teed off that you're going just as we're expecting contractors to come in and redo the roof. It's going to be hard to make sure I'm there when they arrive and when they leave. And I know this is the kind of thing that's triggered some of our worst arguments. But I accept that the house is my responsibility, too, and you're right that you've paid more attention to it so far than I have. So I'll make sure I'm there, and there's even a chance I won't blow up at you in the usual way when, inevitably, they screw up. . . .''

Mark sighed deeply and summed up: ''The needy kid in me has a very strong voice. I know that when I appear to be begging too much it can shove you away. But I now realize that we *both* crave reassurance. I will try to give you as much as you need, or at least as much as I can.''

So, what happened when Julia went to Chicago?

They kept to their phone dates. Julia did—most days, anyway—keep her dream journal, and Mark and she actually laughed as she talked about some of her dreams, which were pretty surreal (''You looked so strange with green hair walking on stilts through my mother's bedroom. . . .''). But because of some quickly canceled and rescheduled meetings, Julia couldn't always get to the phone as planned. Mark freaked out a couple times. One conversation reverted to their old, tense standoff, but Julia called Mark right back and allowed them both to get back on track. Julia did see Charles; she had to sit next to him at a lunch date with four other people. She said she was nervous but polite and distant and, somehow, in her new resolve to reconnect with Mark, she had lost all feeling for Charles. ''I couldn't imagine why he'd seemed so seductive the first time,'' she said. Mark blew up at the contractors who were late nearly every day and made him miss some important business meetings of his own, but he managed not to blow up at Julia. In fact, they were able to laugh about it. A couple of times Mark could feel himself getting "strained": "I couldn't always block out the old fear that maybe Julia wasn't telling me the whole truth about Charles." A couple of times Julia felt the old urge to shut down, to keep a lid on her feelings, and resisted telling Mark about "everything," but they, in Julia's words, "pushed through" and were able to connect satisfyingly nearly the whole time Julia was away. "Again," she said, "we didn't just swallow our anger and reach a kind of tense compromise. We pushed through back to our love for each other."

The larger picture, now, has become much better for Mark and Julia. They sometimes think it hasn't (remember the one-step-forward/two-steps-backward quality of any real growth). But friends of theirs have commented on how comfortable they now are as a couple to spend time with (they didn't use to be). Both sets of in-laws are getting along better with Mark and Julia, too.

An important point: they're also each getting along better with colleagues at work. "These listening principles don't work only between lovers," Julia says. "They've given me incredible clarity about what my boss is trying to say, what just about anyone who talks to me is trying to say. This works across the board—especially across the board of directors at my firm!"

A greater sense of comfort and peace radiates from Julia and Mark, both separately and together—punctuated, of course, by some of the old stormy explosions and disagreements. But both of them now tell me that they feel they can't "go back." "Now that we've built all these bridges to each other," Mark says, "how can I pretend I don't know Julia, or pretend that she doesn't know me? I know that we *do* know each other. And that there's always a way to get back to that knowledge, even after the worst blowup. We know how to listen to each other now. We know how to get back to the love."

Now let's briefly take a look at our personality types to see what they're likely to face, and how they're likely to fare, in "building a bridge."

Building a Bridge: A Plan for Every Personality Type

The Somatizer. If you're a somatizer, as much as you've enjoyed basking in the unaccustomed warmth of Step Six, you may panic at the idea of opening your mouth to speak in Step Seven—or, if you're the speaker, closing your mouth to listen to your partner. It's very hard to hold onto the probably very fragile optimism you've managed to cultivate up until now: the warning signs of a migraine could be near.

Understand, first of all, that this is a very difficult step for you, and be compassionate about the reasons why. Step Seven may seem to be torture. It asks you to *say what you feel*—albeit in your partner's terms—when what you've been doing, probably for a lifetime, is taking out your feelings on your body, keeping them inside, keeping them away from anyone else. Your impulse will be to be irrational—to get away at all costs, to say anything just to be done with talking, to get up and leave the room without warning.

One somatizing client was helped by a visualization exercise. You might be, too. She saw, in her mind, a huge, towering, thick stone wall in front of her, stretching as far she could see to the left and right, massive, impenetrable. Then she allowed herself to see a door in the wall, a door she moved toward slowly, a door she told herself she could open, and which would allow her to get past the wall. "For a long time," she said, "all I could do was approach the door. But one day I opened it. And I walked through. And I was all right.'' Now when she approaches the seventh step with her husband, she allows herself to visualize that door in the wall, approach it, open it, then open her eyes and talk to her husband about her real feelings.

By now you know you don't want to spend the rest of your life blocked by your own wall. Take the cue from this woman, and imagine a door in it, a door you can open. It will turn out, I promise, to be something you've been yearning to do all along. It will help you to speak, to let out all you've been holding in. The seventh step, once so feared, will turn out to be your greatest salvation. Be patient, but keep approaching that door.

The Overly Cheery. If you're overly cheery, you're probably resisting the seventh step as fearfully as the somatizer. Now you're supposed to reveal what you've been hiding: the dark side of yourself. It will seem, as you approach Step Seven, as if you'll be giving up all control and power, giving your partner data he or she can use against you! You hate stating your own needs, even if stated empathically, because you're afraid your partner will reject you once those needs are known. Even after creating the best possibility of being understood—which you have done in the preceding six steps—it may turn out, after all, that your own needs cannot be met.

So, what do you do in the face of that grim possibility? Brush it all away, put the mask of cheer back on, let everyone know that it "doesn't really matter"?

It does matter. The inducement is that you're pushing your edge of growth by revealing your vulnerable side to your partner. You don't have to protect yourself from being disappointed; by learning to accept your partner's dark side, you've experienced a great lesson: you can survive the expression of need, of pain, even of despair. Step Seven will always represent a leap, but it's not as great a leap as you fear. You're already nearly there, simply from the work you've done in the preceding steps.

But what if your needs, once expressed, *are* met? This can present a peculiar problem, too. You may feel so "accepted" by your partner when you finally express your needs that you may overreact and think that this marks the end of crisis forevermore. Now you can be cheery for the rest of your days, secure in your having solved everything! This, however, is just another way of shutting down. There will always be more pain, more comfort, more dark, more light. Congratulate yourself that you're learning, slowly, to meet all categories of feeling and experience head-on. Allow yourself, when you need to, to cry. The tears will stop, be replaced by laughter, and then come back again and be replaced again. The seventh step can teach you to weather whatever comes up.

The Perfectionist. At this moment, if you're a perfectionist, you're happy—you've had a perfect moment of empathy in the sixth step! You should be able to continue just as gratefully into the seventh step. You've always liked talking about your needs in the past; now you have a much more effective way of doing it. By listening to your partner with less criticism, you have learned to hear a different kind of "language" and thus are now able to talk about your own feelings in a much more rounded, soft, and realistic way. This gives you a better chance of having your needs heard and, possibly, met: your partner, at the very least, will be able to understand why you have the needs you do, because you're expressing them in his or her own terms.

Of course, you will probably always feel uncomfortable with "ambiguity": your impulse to quantify, to be accurate about the facts, will never go away—nor does it have to. Perhaps you can simply accept that you've come up with a new "fact" to add to the picture: the fact of emotional vulnerability, changeability—the predictability of the unpredictable! Accept that you've added a new dimension to your understanding of human experience. And you've found a "perfect" means of exploring this dimension: these seven steps.

The Blamer has been waiting all throughout these steps to get to this moment—when he can finally speak! However, to the blamer, "speaking" has almost automatically meant "accusing." Now you have a choice to adopt a different perspective. For one thing, after experiencing the empathy you've felt for your partner in the sixth step, you realize your partner is someone you didn't know he or she was: a *friend*. An ally. Someone against whom you don't have to defend yourself. Someone to whom you don't have to justify every breath you take. A friend is someone who likes you, who cares about what you feel, who wants your desires to be fulfilled, someone who has all the human qualities that are in you as well.

Now that you can see your partner more as a friend, you can learn to trust and make use of this friendship. Realize that there is more good will between you than there was before. This alone will probably take the sting out of what you were going to say: no longer will you feel the automatic reflex to "accuse." Really, you're just allowing a process to occur that, in a sense, *wants* to happen: like every other personality type we've explored, like every human being in the world, we want to be rid of what blocks us. This is your chance to shed some of your own load. Step Seven feeds on good will: now, miraculously, because of all the other steps, you will probably find you have good will to spare. Talk to your partner as an ally, someone who actually *wants* to see that your needs are met. The blaming instinct, for the moment, will abate—very possibly disappear. (It will come back, but now you know you can recognize and deal with it.)

The Advice-Giver. If you're an advice-giver, the seventh step isn't easy. This is the time to reveal your needs, and the strong temptation will be to couch your needs in terms you think will "help" your partner. This is slippery: you may think you're building a bridge this way—you're using your partner's terms, aren't you?—but you're not. The seventh step is a time to stay close to your *own* needs, not to convince your partner how fulfilling your needs will help your partner, too. (It *may,* but that's not the point.)

Make a pact with yourself. Silently repeat, as often as it takes to sink in, the following mantra before speaking in the seventh step: *"I've heard your needs. Now here's what I need."* For a change, allow *yourself* to come out front and be the one who requires some care and attention. As before, you'll probably experience a deep relief. You're doing what you've always longed to do: let your partner know how you feel. But now you realize you can do this "nakedly": you don't have to look out for your partner all the time; sometimes it's all right to look out for yourself, even to tell your partner you'd like him or her to look out a little bit for you, too. Your specific request also takes the burden off the other person to be a mind reader. It shifts the power between you so that it's shared more equally. It allows a more adult love to flower.

The Moralist. After Step Six, if you're a moralist, you've finally shattered the black-and-white view of the world to which you had always subscribed. Your main protection came from pitting the good guys against the bad guys, but now you know it's not so simple. So, for the moment, you've let go of that defense. You can now say: "My partner is human. So am I."

You'll recall the Roman Catholic woman I mentioned in Step Three who was devastated to find that her husband had been divorced, devastated because her morality made divorce an unconscionable sin. She was able to "shelve" this strict prohibitory belief for the time it took to go through these steps. By Step Seven, she found herself saying this to her husband: "We need to be together to find a solution. The solution can only come if we keep all our channels open. I realize I had always half-consciously known or suspected you were divorced—I'd just selectively blocked out the details until now. I remember a party where some old friends of yours asked you about alimony. I must have simply pushed that down back then. And yet I was able to live with you, happily, for all these years. I guess I have to realize that my desire to be with you is in conflict with my old beliefs. I'm willing to hold those beliefs up to a new light. I'm not sure, yet, what I will end up changing, or what I feel we'll have to do. But I want to be with you as I grapple with these feelings and thoughts.''

The moralist can be reborn in these Seven Steps: like the perfectionist, the moralist comes to see that reality is a much more ambiguous business than he or she had imagined. You still face having to make decisions, even if reality *isn't* black and white; but you can learn to make those decisions with more of an open heart. Beliefs, if they don't serve you, can change. You learn that you may have more options than you thought you had.

The Infinite Circle

As we've seen, an intangible requirement of succeeding at the seventh step is good will with benefit of the doubt thrown in. As we discovered when we looked at the sixth step and its call for empathy, you don't generally get this far without feeling a great deal of good will; for one thing, you won't have had the patience to stick it out this long. Without love, you'll generally experience a falling-off in the steps pretty early on.

But what if you know there is love and you still have a bad relapse to some behavior you know is damaging to your relationship? What if, for example, Julia had ended up back in bed with Charles on that Chicago trip?

Mark and Julia would still have had a chance. The process of the seven steps is always open to them: you can always recoup and start over. You cannot erase the progress you've made, the deep emotional understanding you have now of yourself and your partner, of your motives and how you interact. Relapses certainly don't help; if they're perceived to be damaging enough, they can ultimately stamp out love. But you can also recover from them, via the same seven steps that first revealed the depth and complexity of your and your partner's personalities, motives, and love for each other.

What you can count on discovering, relapse or not, is that your partner is always more than you bargained for. And so, for that matter, are you! You are both larger and more complex beings than you realized at the start. You also learn that you're always dealing with each other's unfinished business. One of our major life challenges, as adults, is to *finish* this unfinished business, to recognize and repair the damage we experienced as children—what we couldn't (or weren't equipped to) deal with then. These steps are a wonderful mechanism to allow you to look at, sort out, and work with this unfinished business, with the partner you most probably chose because he or she in some way *represented* the central dilemma you still want to solve. You've married someone, in other words, who can really teach you how to overcome your ancient childhood obstacles. This is because our partners inevitably remind us of the most difficult qualities we found in our parents and/or siblings. What an opportunity this is! Using these steps, you can finally devise effective ways to stop and change old repetitive scenes that impede you. You can discover a new feeling of competence, and an opportunity to push your "edge of growth" a little further out. Once you've experienced the self-honesty asked for in these steps, you can no longer lie to yourself about your own part, your own complicity, in the problems as well as the joys of your relationship with your partner, and in your life generally. Relationships, you find, are an infinite circle: you affect him, he affects you, and on it goes. Each of you shapes the other's behavior for better or worse. This is not to ignore the fact that you each come to your relationship with your own, separate personalities and life experiences. But you discover that your behavior has an *effect* on your partner, on the world around you, and as you change your behavior, you change your effect.

The purpose of these seven steps is to give you as much control over this effect as possible; to allow each of you to express yourselves completely and fully, so that you truly know, when you say or hear the phrase "I love you," just who the "I" and the "you" really are.

Index

Abandonment
  fear of, advice-givers and,
    117
  separation and, 73
Abuse
  sexual, 77, 98
  somatizer and, 113
Acting reflexively, 7
Activating the inner ear, 25, 76,
    87–102
Adaptations, childhood tensions
    and, 104
Addictions, 39, 61
Advice-Giver, The
  activating the inner ear,
    99–100
  building a bridge, 149–150
  crossing the street, 64–65
  engaging the outer ear, 81–82
  expressing tension, 40–41
  learning to enjoy love,
    133–134
  reaching for the past, 117–118

Affirming your love, 121–137
Anger, divorce and, 123–124
Anxiety. See Tension
Assumptions, associations and,
    110

Bipolar disorder, 78
Black-and-white world, 118
Blame
  shame and, 9–10
  understanding nature of, 25
  urge to, 8
Blamer, The
  activating the inner ear, 98–99
  building a bridge, 149
  crossing the street, 63–64
  engaging the outer ear, 80–81
  expressing tension, 40
  learning to enjoy love, 133
  reaching for the past, 116–117
Blowing up, tension and, 51–52
Breathing exercises, 48

Bridge, building a, 25, 139–153
Buber, Martin, 121
Buddhist chanting, 48
Building a bridge, 25, 139–153
Burying and spewing, 35–36

Cease fire, temporary, 56
Cheery, being overly
    activating the inner ear, 96–97
    building a bridge, 147–148
    crossing the street, 59–62
    engaging the outer ear, 78–79
    expressing tension, 39
    learning to enjoy love,
        131–132
    reaching for the past, 113–114
Childhood
    memories of, connecting with,
        103–120
    roots of shame, 9
    repairing damage of, 152
Circle
    filling the, 70–73
    infinite, 151–153
    -of-light visualization, 53–54
Climatic visualization, 97
Coercion, 28
Communication, seven steps to,
    25–28
Compassion, 126
Complex reality, 119
Compulsive attention to detail.
    See Perfectionist, The

Compulsive eater, 59–61
Conflict and silence, 32–35
Consciousness, bringing
    childhood memories to,
    103–120
Control, losing, 45–46
Cooling down, 45–68
Crossing the street, 25–26,
    45–68
    books on, 68
Cultural differences, tension
    tactics and, 42

Dampening the powder keg,
    51–54
Defensiveness, blame and,
    9–10
Detachment
    defeating "fight or flight,"
        69–70
    empathizing through, 25,
        121–137
    from reflex, 45–68
Detail, excessive attention to.
    See Perfectionist, The
Divorce as a result, 123–124
Dream, hearing the, 88–91,
    115

Eating compulsively, 59–61
Emotional abuse, somatizer and,
    113

Empathizing through
    detachment, 25, 108,
    121–137
Engaging the outer ear, 25,
    69–86
est, 48

Facts, obsession with, 62–63,
    79–80, 97–98, 114, 148
Fear
    of intimacy, 9–10
    pushing through the, 58
Feeling your partner's
    communication,
    121–137
"Fight or flight" reflexes,
    defeating, 69–70
Free association, 119
Freud, Sigmund, 115

Gestalt, 48
Good will, necessity of, 151
Guilt, blame and, 63–64, 80–81,
    99, 116, 133

Hearing the dream, 88–91,
    115
Honesty, tension and, 35
Horizontal vs. vertical thinking,
    97
Hurting as a motive, 55–56

I/thou relationship, 121, 139
Identifying with your partner,
    121–137
Illness, channeling feelings into,
    38–39, 57–59, 76–78,
    95–96, 112–113
Imagination, listening with,
    87–102
Infinite Circle, 151–153
Inner ear, activating, 25, 76,
    87–102
Intimacy, fear of, 9–10
Intimate communication, seven
    steps to, 25–28
Intuition, listening with, 87–102
Irrational rage, divorce and,
    123–124
Isolation, pain of, 26–27

Judgemental behavior
    activating the inner ear,
        100–102
    building a bridge, 150–151
    crossing the street, 65–66
    engaging the outer ear, 82–84
    expressing tension, 41–42
    learning to enjoy love,
        134–135
    listening without, 69–86
    reaching for the past, 118–119

Kelly, George, 69

Language, expressing yourself
using your partner's,
139–153
Listening
importance of, 26–27
with intuition, 87–102
without judging, 69–86
Living in the moment, 17, 25
Logic, listening and, 88
Losing control, 45–46
Love, affirming, 121–137

Manic depression. *See* Bipolar
disorder
Martyrdom, stance of, 125
Me vs. we, 7–28
Meditation
activating the inner ear with,
98
benefits of, 43
books on, 68
crossing the street with,
46–49, 53, 60, 63, 67
See also Visualization
Meditative "space," 27
Memories, bringing to
consciousness, 103–120
Merge, urge to, 136
Moment, living in the, 17,
25
Moralist, The
activating the inner ear,
100–102

building a bridge, 150–151
crosssing the street, 65–66
engaging the outer ear, 82–84
expressing tension, 41–42
learning to enjoy love,
134–135
reaching for the past, 118–119
Motivations, understanding,
10–25

Nagging, handling, 60–61

Obsessive/compulsive disorders,
39–40
Outer ear, engaging, 25, 69–86
Overly Cheery, The
activating the inner ear,
96–97
building a bridge, 147–148
crossing the street, 59–62
engaging the outer ear, 78–79
expressing tension, 39
learning to enjoy love,
131–132
reaching for the past, 113–114
Oversleeping, 61
Overworking, 61

Past, reaching for the, 25,
103–120
Peale, Norman Vincent, 59

Perfectionist, The, 30, 33
    activating the inner ear, 97–98
    building a bridge, 148
    crossing the street, 61–63
    engaging the outer ear, 79–80
    expressing tension, 39–40
    learning to enjoy love,
        132–133
    reaching for the past,
        114–116
Personal construct, 69
Personality categories
    activating the inner ear,
        95–102
    building a bridge, 146–151
    crossing the street, 57–66
    engaging the outer ear, 76–84
    learning to enjoy love,
        130–135
    reaching for the past,
        112–119
    tension tactics and, 38–41
Physical ailments, channeling
        feelings into, 38–39,
        57–59, 76–78, 95–96,
        112–113
Playwright, becoming a, 10–25
Preconceived ideas, 119
Primal scream therapy, 48
Procrastination, 61

Reaching for the past, 25,
        103–120

Recognizing tension, 25–26,
        29–44, 38–41
Reflex
    acting by, 7
    defeating "fight or flight,"
        69–70
    detaching yourself from,
        45–68
Reframing your thinking,
        139–153
Relaxations, discovering, 43,
        48–49, 67. See also
        Meditation; Visualization
Resistance, connecting with
        childhood tensions and,
        103
Ritual behavior, superstitiously
        adhering to, 39–40
Roles, switching, 55–57

Safe communications "space,"
        70
Scapegoats. See Blame
Scuba diving vs. snorkeling,
        91–95, 129
Self-compassion, 52
Self-sufficiency, silence and, 33
Sensitizing yourself to tension,
        25–26, 29–44
    tension tactics, 38–41
Separation
    abandonment and, 73
    as a result, 123–124

Seven steps to intimate
    communication, 25–28
Sexual abuse, 77, 98
Shame
    blame and, 9–10
    tender private information
        and, 88
Shaw, George Bernard, 24
Silence and conflict, 32–35
Socrates, 24
Somatizer, The
    activating the inner ear,
        95–96
    building a bridge, 146–147
    crossing the street, 57–59
    engaging the outer ear, 76–78
    expressing tension, 38–39
    learning to enjoy love,
        130–131
    reaching for the past, 112–113
Spewing and burying, 35–36
Staying in the room, 46–50, 61
Street, crossing the, 25–26,
    45–68
Stress
    sensitizing yourself to, 25–26,
        29–44
    tension tactics, 38–41
Substance abuse, 39, 61
Supersensitivity, 52

Switching roles, 55–57
Sympathy, need for, 77

Temper, losing your, 45–46
Tender, private information, 88
Tension
    recognizing, 25–26, 29–44
    tactics, 38–41
Time out, calling, 56
Truth, real vs. emotional,
    114–115

Venting, 55
Vertical vs. horizontal thinking,
    97
Visualization, 53–54, 61, 67
    climatic, 97
    somatizer crossing the bridge
        with, 146–147
    See also Meditation

Whirling dervish and tension,
    35, 42
Withdrawal, 46–50
Workplace, applying listening
    principles to, 145
Wounding words, 55–56

www.ingramcontent.com/pod-product-compliance
Lightning Source LLC
Chambersburg PA
CBHW061244280526
45784CB00002B/631